Do's and Taboos of Preparing for Your Trip Abroad

Other books by the authors:

By Roger E. Axtell

Do's and Taboos Around the World: A Guide to International
    Behavior, Third Edition
Do's and Taboos of International Trade: A Small Business
    Primer, Second Edition
Do's and Taboos of Hosting International Visitors
Gestures: The Do's and Taboos of Body Language Around
    the World
Do's and Taboos of Public Speaking

By John P. Healy

International Marketing: The Hospitality Guide to
    Attracting and Serving International Travelers

Do's and Taboos of Preparing for Your Trip Abroad

Roger E. Axtell
John P. Healy

Illustrations by Mike Fornwald

John Wiley & Sons, Inc.

New York • Chichester • Brisbane • Toronto • Singapore

To our wives, Mitzi and Peggy,
without whom we would never be prepared for anything!

Copyright © 1994 by Roger E. Axtell and John P. Healy
Published by John Wiley & Sons, Inc.

Library of Congress Cataloging-in-Publication Data:

Axtell, Roger E.
  Do's and taboos of preparing for your trip
  abroad / Roger E. Axtell
      p. cm.
  Includes index
  ISBN 0-471-02567-4

Printed in the United States of America

10 9 8 7 6 5 4 3 2 1

CONTENTS

Introduction   ix

1 Planning Your Itinerary   1

Doing Your Homework • Selecting a Travel
Agent • Package Tours: Packed In or Paradise? •
Going Solo • Adventure Trips • Resources for
Special Needs

2 Transportation Options   17

Air Travel • Selecting Your Seat on an Airline •
Cruising the High Seas • Riding the Rail •
Driving on Your Own

3 Passports and Visas   32

Your Passport: The Best Proof • Applying for a
Passport • Passports for Children • How to Get a
Passport in an Emergency • Amending Your
Passport • What to Do if Your Passport Is Lost
or Stolen • How to Protect Your Passport •
Obtaining Visas • Tourist Cards

4 Selecting the Right Accommodations   42

Types of Accommodations • Off the Beaten
Path • Making Reservations—The Smart Way •
What Is and Isn't Included? • Concierge: Friend or
Foe? • Are Special Services Available? • Phoning
Home—Bargain or Bonanza? • Don't Forget to
Send a Postcard • Making Sure You're Plugged In •
A Few Final Thoughts about Lodging

5 Money Matters Matter   54

Planning Your Monetary Needs • Credit and Charge
Cards • Traveler's Checks • Traveler's Check
Safety • Foreign Currency • Accessing Your Cash: The
Age of ATM Withdrawals • Emergency Funds •

The Value-Added Tax (VAT) • Preparing for
the Customs Process

6 Staying Healthy 66

Before You Go • A Shot in the Arm • Your Personal
Prescriptions • Avoiding Illness and Injury When
You Travel • Prevention Is the Best Tactic • If You
Do Get Sick Abroad • Combating Jet Lag

7 Traveling Safely 76

Safety Tips before You Leave Home • Safety on
Airplanes • Safety Do's and Don'ts When Staying
in a Hotel • Protecting Yourself against Theft •
Other Safety Do's and Don'ts • Help from the
U.S. Government • Recommended Reading on
Traveling Safely

8 A Cultural Survival Kit 86

Coping with Cultural Differences • Bathrooms
of the World • Greetings • Dining •
Punctuality • Gift Giving • Tipping •
Recommended Reading List

9 Coping with a Foreign Language 96

How to Communicate Effectively • Learning
Some Foreign Phrases

10 Business Trips 102

The Role of the U.S. Department of Commerce •
Tips for Preparing a Business Trip Abroad •
Recommended Reading

11 Insurance 108

Types of Insurance • How Policies Can Be
Obtained • Where to Start • Insurance Companies

12 Luggage and Packing 118

Which Type of Luggage Is Best? • Tips for
Backpackers • Security and Your Luggage •

Packing • What Clothing to Pack? • Preparing a
Carry-On Survival Kit • What to Wear En Route
• What to Do about Damaged or Lost Luggage

Appendix A	Additional Reading	131
Appendix B	Tourist Information Offices around the World	133
Appendix C	Foreign Voltage Guide	139
Appendix D	Travel Bookstores	140
Index		146

ACKNOWLEDGMENTS

At the risk of sounding redundant, there were several people who helped us *prepare* this compendium on *how to prepare*. With one of us working on two other books simultaneously and the other struggling to keep a fledgling business afloat, the support, insight, and can-do attitude of these folks helped us pull it all together.

First and foremost, our thanks to Susan Levine, whose enthusiasm for this project was contagious. From our very first content meeting right down to the last day of proofreading, Susan's crack organizational skills and thoughtful recommendations were invaluable. *Muchas gracias,* Susan.

Others who helped us to research, plan chapters, and prepare the manuscript included Rob Friedman, Michele Kelley, Frances Kraft, Carol McCarthy, and Yolanda Booth. *Grazie,* for all your efforts!

Special acknowledgment must also be given to the members of the Citibank team who enabled us to create *Do's and Taboos of Preparing for Your Trip Abroad* as a concept in the first place. The vision of Elaine Buss, Jeff Kraft, and Margie Ogawa brought the first iteration of these words to the thousands of Americans who were asking where they could find information on *preparing.* For your vision and confidence in us—*merci beaucoups!*

Danke Schoen to the folks at John Wiley & Sons; Kitt Allan, for her cooperation in getting the Citibank promotion off the ground; and PJ Dempsey, for supporting our notion to turn this work into a book.

Finally, our gratitude to those other professionals who lent a hand along the way: travel consultants Su Dwyer, David A. Fleig, and Lori J. Kidd; insurance counselor Charles Elliott; and finally, to world traveler and scholar Richard W. Holznecht.

ROGER E. AXTELL
JOHN P. HEALY

INTRODUCTION

We Americans apparently have itchy feet. According to the U.S. Travel and Tourism Administration, *one in five* Americans traveled outside the United States in 1993. That's close to 50 million people.

Furthermore, the number of outgoing Americans keeps rising each year. There was a 6 percent jump from 1992 to 1993, and a 43 percent increase over 10 years ago.

Our itchy feet can be costly, too. American voyagers spent approximately $66 billion (including transportation costs) on travels outside the United States in 1993. That's a 16.7 percent increase over 1992. Also, according to 1990 surveys, the average traveler spends $2,305 per trip.

The typical traveler leaving the United States spends 73 days in the *planning stages* of travel and books airline reservations an average of 44 days before actual departure. During this four-month period, the traveler is confronted with dozens, scores, even hundreds of questions and decisions about how to travel economically, enjoyably, and productively.

This book is designed to help answer those questions and assist you in making those decisions whether you are traveling as a tourist, a student, or a business person. And whether you're a perfectionist who likes to anticipate every contingency, or a procrastinator who dislikes preparing for *any* trip, this book will make your preparation easier.

The forerunner of this book was a 12-page pamphlet published by Citibank World Wallet in May 1993. We prepared that pamphlet for Citibank and created a plan to promote and publicize it.

More than 25,000 of the pamphlets were produced and then distributed through Citibank branches and via direct mail. Citibank also established a toll-free Hotline that allowed callers to request the pamphlet.

The Hotline offered a second feature: The caller could ask a specific question about overseas travel. Over six months' time, the Hotline received more than 10,000 phone requests for the booklet and almost as many specific questions about world travel, many of them sensible and predictable, others wild and off-beat. Those questions—and the answers that were provided by the authors during that time—have been used as grist for this book.

We hasten to emphasize that preferences, tastes, and decisions regarding overseas travel are a very *subjective* process.

For instance, Roger Axtell names London, Hong Kong, and the Egyptian Pyramids at Giza as his all-time favorite, memorable destinations. John Healy, on the other hand, favors the European Continent—especially Rome, Paris, and Geneva.

Axtell's choice in airplane seating is always "Next to the window and near the front." Healy says, "I always select aisle seating in the smoking section, if available." And for Axtell, "There is no such thing as arriving too early at an airport," whereas Healy usually rushes to board as the jetway door is about to close.

Both are inveterate travelers, and each brings a special "generational viewpoint" to the information and tips in this book.

Axtell began his business travels in 1956, crisscrossing the United States in a propellered DC-3 corporate aircraft on special assignment for Sears, Roebuck & Co. He later joined The Parker Pen Co. where he served until his retirement 30 years later as Vice President, Worldwide Marketing. In his career at Parker, and since his retirement in 1986, he has lived and traveled overseas for over 30 years. This has caused him to write five books on international travel and behavior. In addition to his writing, he also travels on the professional speaking circuit, informing and entertaining audiences in the United States and overseas with stories and lessons about international protocol, behavior, goofs, and gaffes, and "how to make rude gestures in 22 countries without realizing it."

His Number One travel peeve? "It's when airline passengers in the seat in front of me suddenly recline their seats with the speed and impact of a shotgun, effectively kneecapping me for the rest of the journey."

Healy, on the other hand, brings the viewpoint of the "thirty-something" generation. A public relations executive for more than 12 years and currently Managing Partner of Prescott▼Healy Company Ltd. in Chicago, Healy's travels have included assignments for such organizations as Walgreen Co., Citicorp, the Miss America Organization, Kayser-Roth Hosiery, the makers of No Nonsense pantyhose, and an international health care corporation. He is also the author of *International Marketing: The Hospitality Guide to Attracting and Serving International Travelers,* published by the American Hotel & Motel Association.

His most memorable travel experience: A year spent commuting between his native Chicago and Washington, D.C., where he served a one-year appointment to the U.S. Departments of Commerce and Transportation, which included a three-week tour of eight European capitals.

"Know thyself," admonishes the Oracle of Apollo at Delphi—and not only is the advice still good, but it's the first step in preparing to travel abroad. Our tastes in travel are as varied as our tastes in friends, and before embarking on a complex process of choosing from myriad travel options, ask yourself this simple question: *"What will I like best?"*

Then scratch those itchy feet. You'll never regret it.

CHAPTER **1**

Planning Your Itinerary

After sifting through a mountain of travel promotions, Joe and Dolores could barely contain their excitement as they dialed their travel agent. "Oh, I know exactly what kind of trip you're looking for," chirped the voice on the other end of the line. "I can get you an M or Q fare, but the hotel only offers a full American Plan. If you travel off-peak, I can get a lower rack rate on a Continental Plan on connecting flights there and back." Scratching their heads, Joe and Dolores decided to contact a tour operator they'd heard of instead. "I think I have an independent package, or a city package, or a stay-put package," said the operator. "But you'd probably be better off with an escorted package that's all-inclusive." Confused but undaunted, the couple decided to work out the details themselves by calling a few hotels in the cities they'd selected. "Oui, I've got zee Amurican Plan or just zee European Plan, eef you preefer," said the first reservation manager they reached. "But would you like zee pension or zee demi-pension rate?" In the end, Joe and Dolores spent their vacation fixing up their basement.

In the exploding galaxy of travel options, you can find a star that's exactly right for you. As long as you know *what* you're looking for. As Joe and Dolores began to plan their trip, they should have taken a few minutes to answer the following questions. Begin your planning by asking yourself:

- How long a trip are you planning?
- How much time are you willing to spend on travel to and from your destination(s)?
- What is the purpose of the trip: sightseeing, relaxation, business, visiting friends/relatives?
- What climate, terrain, attractions, and level of activity do you prefer?
- Do you prefer luxury surroundings, roughing it, or something in between?
- When can you go?
- How much can you afford to spend on the *entire* trip?

Those few minutes might be the best way to begin to clarify which of the various options are for you.

1

Regardless of your preferences, give yourself enough time to plan thoroughly, make arrangements yourself, or work with a travel agent. Starting early also enables you to take advantage of travel discounts (such as lower off-peak season rates on hotels, car rentals, cruises, entertainment, and other aspects of your trip).

TRAVEL TIP   Certain travel documents should be checked right away, such as passports and visas, immunization records, International Driving Permit, and other documents that require long lead times. Subsequent chapters in this book detail what you need to do. ■

DOING YOUR HOMEWORK

The single most important aspect of preparing to travel is *research*—from choosing destinations and travel arrangements to learning about the customs and protocol of those countries you plan to visit. The more information you gather up front, the better prepared you'll be to plan your trip and make sure everything goes smoothly and safely.

• The first things to decide are where you want to go, when are the best times to go, and how long you'll spend in each location. Start by visiting your local library or bookstore. For travel brochures and more detailed tourist information, contact travel agents, individual country tourist information offices, international airlines, and foreign embassies or consulates here in the United States.

• Learn as much as you can about your destinations—the customs and the native language. Also, check for the dates of national and religious holidays of your destinations to make sure they don't interfere with your travel plans. Read Chapters 8 and 9 in this book, and then peruse bookstores and libraries for phrase and guidebooks and tapes.

• Gather free information from the U.S. government on traveling abroad. Two excellent pamphlets to get you started are the U.S. State Department's *Background Notes,* which provides current information on various countries' customs, culture, geography, history and government, economy and political conditions, and *Tips for Travelers,* which covers currency regulations, customs, and other general travel tips in individual country pamphlets. Contact the Superintendent of Documents, U.S. Government Printing Office, Washington, DC 20402, (202)783-3238, or check your local library or U.S. Government Printing Bookstore.

• Determine the best method of making your arrangements, choosing from travel agents, tour operators, cruise lines or other professionals, or doing it on your own. *No matter which method of travel planning you choose, be sure to work far enough ahead so that you're not wasting precious time on arrangements that could have been made before you left home.*

SELECTING A TRAVEL AGENT

Consulting a travel agent will cut the hassles associated with traveling and will save you time and money. More than 200,000 U.S. travel agents account for almost 90 percent of airline ticket, cruise, and package tour sales, more than half of all car rentals, and one quarter of all hotel bookings made each year. Travel agents not only make your plane and hotel arrangements, they'll also help customize a trip to meet your specific needs, offer advice, and help untangle travel-related problems. Best of all, because most agents work on commissions from service providers—usually 10 percent—they do not charge travelers for their services.

Types of Travel Agents

• *Full-Service Agencies* are what most of us think of when we hear the words "travel agent." Making their money on commissions, they range from giants like Thomas Cook to Mom & Pop operations that win customers by providing tailored service and personal attention.

• *Specialists (Destination Agents)* focus on a specific travel niche, such as business travel, leisure travel, tours of Italy, hiking/camping, cruises, or renting villas. Also known as "destination agents," they work on commission like most travel agents.

• *Rebaters* return part of their commission to travelers, and target those interested in the lowest price available for airfares, hotels, cruises, and package tours. They deal with people who know exactly where and how they're going to travel. You call with the details, and the agency finds the best price.

• *Fee-Based Agents* do not receive commissions from service providers, but charge clients a fee for their service instead. Very few travel agencies work on this basis.

Travel agents typically use a central reservation system to access and book arrangements. Such systems provide a broad range of providers, prices, and options, which ultimately enable them to offer the best price at the best times for you.

Steps in Choosing a Travel Agent.   To choose a travel agent who's right for you, follow these five steps:

1. *Know yourself.* You'll be better able to select and evaluate an agent if you know exactly what kind of travel experience you want. If you're dreaming of touring the vineyards of France, you'll want an agent who is conversant with the country, the wine regions, the best times to go, and so on. Thinking of diving off the Great Barrier Reef? You'll want an agent with a different sea of knowledge.

2. *Cast your net wide.* Choose a travel agent like you would any other service professional: carefully and deliberately. You can check your newspaper's travel section, the yellow pages, or your company's travel agency. But you may do even better if you ask a friend or relative who has similar interests; their recommendation is worth more than any advertisement.

3. *Judge for yourself.* When you meet with a travel agent, grade them on their personal attention and their knowledge as well as the services they offer. It helps if you know what services most agents automatically provide. A good agent will:

• Search for the lowest fares and rates.

• Consider and meet your health-related requirements. For example, they'll arrange for vegetarian or low-cholesterol meals on airline flights and find hotels that offer nonsmoking accommodations.

• Be able to inform you about specific aspects of your trip. Your agent should know about visa requirements, immunizations, climate, political unrest, seasonal rates—and other areas that guidebooks might overlook. One way to check on this point is to ask your agent questions about places with which you're familiar.

• Pay attention to details. Is the material your agent gives you current? Does the agent know your destination and hotel first-hand? Are the train timetables for this year—or 1970? During the time of your trip, are there special events that you should know about?

4. *Choose someone you trust.* Select a travel agent that offers you the level of personal service you want. You can help ensure your own comfort on a trip by feeling comfortable with your agent first.

5. *Check them out.* While only nine states actually license agents, The Institute of Certified Travel Agents certifies those

who've taken an in-depth course and had five years' agency experience. Look for the designation "CTC" (Certified Travel Counselor) after an agent's name, or contact the Institute at 148 Linden St., P.O. Box 812059, Wellesley, MA 02181-0012, (800)542-4282 (or (617)237-0280 in Massachusetts). Two additional organizations to consult are the American Society of Travel Agents (ASTA), 1101 King St., Alexandria, VA 22314, (703)739-2782, and the Association of Retail Travel Agents (ARTA), 1745 Jefferson Davis Highway, Suite 300, Arlington, VA 22202, (800)969-6069. Also check with your local Better Business Bureau to see if consumers have filed any recent complaints against your agent.

Again, often the best recommendations come by word of mouth. If a travel agent has done a great job for a friend, there's a good chance that agent will serve you well, too.

PACKAGE TOURS: PACKED IN OR PARADISE?

The hotel you booked is by the Thames River, but 25 miles from central London. And the day you arrived, the British public transit system went on strike. Hassles like these—always possible—point to the many advantages of package tours.

When you choose a package tour, all the questions, doubts, worries, and mishaps associated with travel are minimized. A package tour offers a variety of travel services purchased in a single arrangement. A typical package might include round-trip transportation, local transportation (and/or car rentals), accommodations, some or all meals, sightseeing, entertainment, taxes, tips, and a variety of other features.

The advantages of a package tour include simplicity, certainty, and cost savings—especially if a charter or discount flight is included. Packages are economical and convenient, and they will take you anywhere from Antarctica to Zimbabwe.

The Four Types of Package Tours

• *Escorted Tours* tend to begin in a major city—like London or Paris—and spend anywhere from one to three weeks going through a country, covering highlights en route. Hotels are usually first class or better, with rooms including baths and showers. On an escorted tour, a guide accompanies the group from the beginning of the tour through boarding for the flight home. Another version, the locally hosted tour, has the group met at each location by a different host.

• *Independent Tours* combine some aspects of an escorted tour—like traveling by motorcoach—with longer stays in one spot. One popular package is the fly/drive tour, which includes your flight, a rental car, a map, and the freedom to go where you want and see what you want. On an independent tour, there's usually a choice of hotels (travelers receive hotel vouchers as confirmation), meal plans, and sightseeing trips in each city, as well as a variety of special excursions, which you pursue on your own.

• *Stay-Put Packages* enable travelers to stay in one place, but remain free to go where they want. A stay-put city package—regardless of the city—usually includes round-trip transfers between the airport and hotel, plus a choice of hotel accommodations in a variety of price ranges. Typical packages include one or two half-day guided tours of the city, passes for local mass transit, and discount cards for shops, museums, and restaurants.

• *Special-Interest Packages* can include any or all aspects of other tour packages, but focus on a specific activity or topic. Such packages can focus on wine or food tasting, religious sites or events, sports, theater, shopping, or bird-watching, and tend to be highly structured and expensive.

More than 300 companies around the world offer tour packages. At the end of this chapter, you'll find a list of a few tour companies and the types of tours they offer to get you started.

Do your homework to determine which tour to choose; begin with the same exercise of writing down exactly what you want out of your trip. Take time to research your destination. Then, as you begin to sift through the brochures offered by tour operators, ask these questions:

• *What's included?* Does the tour price include airfare or other transportation, meals, transfers, taxes, baggage handling, tips, or any other services? Does the tour originate in your home city, or will you be required to get yourself to another city for departure with a group? Determine the cost including your own travel.

• *Where are we going?* Check the itinerary carefully. If you choose an escorted tour, note the cities you'll actually be visiting, as opposed to those places you'll be driving through. Match the pace with your needs. Is there too much bus travel or too much walking? The right balance of leisure time and structured activity? Find the answers that best suit your tastes.

- *Where are we staying?* Pay close attention to the descriptions and ratings of the hotels. Make sure the accommodations match your expectations, and find out where the hotels are located. If transportation is provided, 10 miles from downtown is probably okay; if you're walking, it's a different story. Also, if you're traveling alone, find out about the single supplement. The prices quoted in most brochures are based on double occupancy (the rate listed for each of two people sharing a double room). If you travel alone, the single supplement can tack quite a bit onto the price.

- *What's for lunch?* And breakfast, dinner, and snacks, for that matter? Like accommodations, meals can be one of the most important parts of the package. Does "some meals included" mean two a day, or just a farewell dinner? Find out how many and what kinds of meals are included. If you want the flexibility of choosing your own meals, you may want to avoid a package that provides every meal.

- *What's the fine print?* Better read it—it can often get hidden underneath the glowing pictures of Mount Fuji or the Eiffel Tower. As you read the section typically labeled *Conditions,* in addition to the previous four questions, ask yourself the following: Do prices vary according to season? Are the prices guaranteed (that is, if prices go up after you book, do you pay more)? Are there cancellation penalties? The *Conditions* page might be the least attractive in the brochure, but the most important to ensure a trip without unpleasant surprises.

Always read the fine print on travel-related contracts or agreements.

TRAVEL TIP When making arrangements, be sure to check your contract *and* ask your travel agent or tour operator about refund/cancellation provisions—especially in the event the tour does not meet your expectations. ■

To qualify the credentials of a tour operator, contact the United States Tour Operators Association (USTOA), 211 E. 51st Street, Suite 12B, New York, NY 10022, (212)944-5727.

USTOA's members, who account for about 80 percent of all tours leaving the United States, *must* conform to several requirements that protect consumers from tour operator bankruptcy or insolvency. Write for USTOA's helpful brochure entitled *How to Select a Package Tour.*

GOING SOLO

After a frustrating chat with the concierge, you discover that the quaint Parisian hotel you had your heart set on for four months is all full. Can it happen to you? Sure—and it will, if you're traveling solo—unless you take the time to research and plan your trip in advance.

There are many reasons to avoid travel agents and package tours, but the truth is, if you're going to plan it yourself, you're going to have to be your own travel professional, and put your own package together.

Luckily for you, there's a wealth of resources at your fingertips. Here are some places to start:

• *The Sunday travel section of your local newspaper.* Most papers will cover a mix of international destinations and specific regions. You'll discover new places and new ways to see old places. You'll also find current, fairly reliable information, accompanied by phone numbers. Don't overlook the ads, either—they often highlight bargains.

• *Bookstores and libraries.* Like this one, there's a plethora of books devoted to travel. If you peruse your local bookstore's travel and reference shelves, you can find a book that appeals directly to your interests, plans, and budget. In addition to books (which minimizes research costs), most libraries also offer a variety of pertinent magazine and newspaper articles, foreign-language publications and tapes, encyclopedias, and videos on various destinations.

• *Travel magazines.* Like newspapers, the magazines are good sources for ideas. Among the most popular: *Caribbean Travel and Life; Conde' Nast Traveler* (which has an investigative tone); *Islands; National Geographic Traveler* (whose suggestions fall in the moderate range); *Outside* (for adventurers); and *Travel & Leisure* (which appeals to upscale travelers).

• *Tourist information offices.* Many countries consider travel and tourism a valuable source of revenue, and their tourist information offices in the United States exist to attract Americans, providing information on everything from cathedrals to cafes. Appendix B lists tourist information offices for many popular destinations.

• *References from family and friends.* As with other kinds of travel, you may find the most helpful information here. Remember, though, to take into account your own interests in accepting a recommendation from someone you know; they may love the quiet of the countryside while you may prefer the bustle of the city.

• *Travel agents.* Even if you plan your own itinerary, choose your own form of transportation, and travel solo, you may still want to enlist an agent to book flights, accommodations, and rental cars. A good travel agent might also provide information and insights that will add to your knowledge—and your fun.

TRAVEL TIP One last piece of advice for those who go solo: Leave a detailed itinerary (with names, addresses, and phone numbers of people and places you'll visit) with friends or relatives at home. Include a photocopy of your passport information page. This way, people can reach you in an emergency. ■

Leaving a detailed copy of your itinerary with a friend or neighbor is always a good idea, but be careful not to go overboard.

ADVENTURE TRIPS

The truth is, we travel not only for fun, but for excitement, romance, and adventure. Whether you're retracing the route of Amelia Earhart, hiking in the footsteps of Sir Edmond Hillary, or diving in search of Atlantis, you'll find a variety of special trips can help fulfill your dreams of adventure.

The possibilities are as vast as your imagination: ballooning, bicycling, camping, canoeing, diving, dogsledding, hang-gliding, hiking, horseback riding, kayaking, mountain climbing, nature treks, safaris, sailing, skiing, skydiving, and windsurfing. See our listing at the end of this chapter for a few of the tour operators who offer such trips, or check your library or bookstore.

Here are some general tips to follow if you're considering an adventure trip:

• *Plan ahead.* Such trips demand even more advance planning than regular ones. You can hike the world's highest peaks only during certain times of the year; you don't want to bike during the rainy season; and in most of the world's diving meccas, the water is clearer during certain months. Transport to remote locales also will take longer than to major cities, so plan accordingly.

• *Compare tours and tour operators.* Special trips can be expensive, so be sure to check all the details. The same tour can differ by thousands of dollars, depending on which operator is offering it. And because many travel companies—especially adventure travel providers—are in business one day and not the next, be sure to check references, confirm specifics up front and receive guarantees for your money.

• *Pay extra attention to your heath.* Traveling in remote and rural areas—as is the case with most adventure trips—demands very specific health and safety precautions. Check with your tour operator or travel agent, your own doctor, and doctors that specialize in travel medicine. If you're injured abroad, the State Department's Citizens' Emergency Center can help, and Travel Assistance International can arrange an emergency evacuation if necessary. See Chapters 6 and 7 for more details on health and safety.

• *Pack the right clothes.* From the tops of mountains to the jungle terrain, extremes of climate in exotic locales require proper clothing. And because on many adventures you'll be carrying your clothing with you, you need to find lightweight clothing that suits the climate or circumstances. Check with your tour operator and with local specialty clothing stores for help in making the right clothing choices.

• *Get the right equipment.* Whether hiking the Himalayas or scuba-diving the Great Barrier Reef, the right equipment can mean the difference between life and death. At the very least, it can mean the difference between enjoyable days and ongoing irritations. Find out the precise requirements for your specific trip and don't scrimp on the equipment.

Remember, you'll also need to transport your gear overseas. Heavier items can be shipped 5 to 10 weeks ahead of time by either U.S. Sea Mail or commercial shipping services. Most airlines will check bicycles, backpacks, surfboards, and other equipment if it weighs less than 80 pounds. Make sure you pack your gear properly, though. A bike, for example, should be placed in a heavy cardboard box without handlebars and front wheel, and with protection around the derailleur (gear shift).

For information on how to get large amounts of equipment to remote locations, contact The Explorers' Club, 46 E. 70th Street, New York, NY 10021, (212)628-8383; or the Expedition Advisory Center, 1 Kensington Gore, London, SW7 2AR England, (011)4471/581-2057.

• *Pack a special travel kit. The Ultimate Adventure Sourcebook* (Turner Publishing, $29.95), one of the best resource books for adventure travel, suggests a kit that includes the following: a flashlight, a small folding umbrella, a small auto-focus camera with zoom lens, a plastic bottle of iodine (as both an antiseptic and water purifier), a travel clock/calculator, a cheap watch, adhesive tape, a good sunblock, and a sewing kit. Also refer to Chapter 12 on Luggage and Packing for more ideas on preparing a survival kit.

• *Expect the unexpected.* Many adventures are even more dependent on forces beyond your control than other travel—nature, machinery, equipment, even politics. Ask about the potential for disruption, and allow extra time to give yourself some leeway in case a problem arises.

• *Do your homework!*—which brings this chapter full circle. While careful research can help ensure a safe and fun-filled adventure, the truth is, *all* travel is an adventure. And that's the point of this chapter: *The time you put in up front will save you time, worry, effort, and money on your trip.* It enables you to get the details out of the way so when you go, you can enjoy the country, the scenery, and the culture you sought to experience.

Along with *The Ultimate Adventure Sourcebook,* two other resources for international adventure trips are *The Big Book of Adventure* by James Simmons (Dutton, $14.95) and *If You Can't Remember Your Last Vacation, You Need This Book* by Laura Greenburg (Thunder Publications, $14.95). Also, for current information on outdoor adventures, call *Patagonia's Guideline* at (800)523-9597, a free service that offers tips on where to go and what outfitters to use.

TRAVEL TIP   For high-tech types, the *Official Recreation Guide* is an on-line directory of outdoor activities offered by more than 1,000 outfitters and tour companies. You can access the database with a PC and modem. Because the scope of information is so broad, it's easier to use if you have a specific adventure and location in mind. For more information, contact the company at 100 Second Street East, 3rd Floor, Whitefish, MT 59937, (800)826-2135. ∎

Three last-minute reminders before you embark on any trip abroad:

1. Review the three essentials: passport, tickets, money. Without these three, you're not going anywhere. With them, you can travel the world, encountering any form of mishap and still be just fine.
2. Leave a copy of your itinerary behind, including *every* stop on your trip, with a close friend or relative so you can be reached in case of an emergency—at home or abroad.
3. Most important of all, *relax!* You're on your way to excitement, adventure, and romance abroad. *Bon voyage!*

Be sure to place the three most important travel tools— passport, tickets, and money— where you can find them.

RESOURCES FOR SPECIAL NEEDS

Following are resources for those planning itineraries that include the elderly, children, or physically disabled persons.

Older Travelers

- The American Association of Retired Persons' (AARP) Travel Experience, 400 Pinnacle Way, Suite 450, Norcross, GA 30071, (800)927-0111, offers information and assistance for solo travelers and group tours.
- Barbi Tours [(800)824-7102] conducts "Lifestyle Explorations" tours for those considering retirement abroad.

- Most major hotel chains provide special discounts to seniors—although some may require that you pay a small membership fee. Check with individual properties at your destination, or contact major hotel chains for information. Also, most hotels offer reduced rates for AARP members (contact AARP at (800)424-3410 for information).

- Several national tour companies offer trips specially designed for seniors, including Grand Circle, (800)321-2835; Saga Holidays, (800)343-0273; Mountain Travel/Sobek, (800)227-2384; Society Expeditions, (800)548-8669; Elderhostel, (617)426-8056; Club Med (800)CLUB-MED, which has a number of properties that offer "Forever Young" vacations for travelers 60 and over.

- Grand Circle Travels publishes a free booklet entitled *Going Abroad: 101 Tips for Mature Travelers*. Contact Grand Circle at 347 Congress Street, Boston, MA 02210, (800)221-2610 or (617)350-7500.

Child Travelers

- The U.S. Department of Transportation offers a free booklet entitled *Kids and Teens in Flight,* which provides guidelines and tips for younger travelers. Write to U.S. Department of Transportation, Office of Consumer Affairs, I-25, Washington, DC 20590, (202)366-2220.

- Travel with Your Children publishes a newsletter for members entitled *Family Travel Times*. Contact TWYCH at 45 W. 18th Street, 7th Floor Tower, New York, NY 10011, (212)206-0688. This organization also offers books and pamphlets, including *Cruising with Children*.

- Check your local library or bookstore for books that specialize in this area. A few to look for include *Travel with Children: A Travel Survival Kit* by Maureen Wheeler (Lonely Planet Publications) and *Trouble-Free Travel with Children: Helpful Hints for Parents on the Go* by Vicki Lansky (Book Peddlers).

- Carousel Press offers a series of guidebooks to help make traveling with children educational and fun. For a listing of the topics available, contact Carousel at P.O. Box 6061, Albany, CA 94706, (510)527-5849 for *The Family Travel Guides Catalog*.

Physically Disabled Travelers

- Mobility International is a network of affiliates that offers advice and assistance on accommodations, wheelchair access, and various travel services. Contact Mobility International USA,

P.O. Box 10767, Eugene, OR 97440, (503)343-1284 (voice/ TDD) for information about services, membership, MIUSA's quarterly newsletter and referral to international affiliates, including England, Germany, Ireland, Italy, and Switzerland. MIUSA also offers a guide book for $16 entitled *A World of Options for the 90s: A Guide to International Educational Exchange, Community Service and Travel for Persons with Disabilities.*

- The Society for the Advancement of Travel for the Handicapped (SATH) works to improve conditions for disabled travelers. The organization is a clearinghouse for information on travel conditions for the disabled throughout the world, and works to create barrier-free environments for handicapped travelers. For membership information, contact SATH at 347 Fifth Avenue, Suite 610, New York, NY 10016, (212)447-SATH.
- For a free list of travel agencies that specialize in tours and trips for the disabled, send a self-addressed, stamped envelope to ACCENT on Living, P.O. Box 700, Bloomington, IL 61702, (309)378-2961. ACCENT also offers several publications for disabled travelers, including a quarterly newsletter for members.
- To obtain a free fact sheet entitled *The Disabled Traveler,* write Office of Consumer Affairs, Department of Transportation, I-25, Washington, DC 20590.

Tour Operators and Types of Tours They Offer

Tour Operators	Escorted	Independent	Stay-Put	Special Interest	Adventure
Abercrombie & Kent, 1520 Kensington Road, Suite 212, Oak Brook, IL 60521, (708)954-2944 in Illinois; (800)323-7308 elsewhere in the United States	X	X	X	X	X
Bennett Tours, 270 Madison Avenue, New York, NY 10016, (800)221-2420	X	X	X		
Bombard Ballon Adventures, 6727 Curran Street, McLean, VA 22101-3804, (800)862-8537	X			X	X
Brendan Tours, 15137 Califa Street, Van Nuys, CA 91411, (800)421-8446	X	X	X		
Brian Moore International, 116 Main Street, Medway, MA 02053, (800)982-2299	X	X	*	**	**
Celtic International, 161 Central Avenue, Albany, NY 12206, (800)833-4373	X	X		**	**
CIE Tours International, 108 Ridgedale Avenue, Morristown, NJ 07960, (800)CIE-TOUR	X	X	X	**	**
Club Med, 40 West 57th Street, New York, NY 10019, (800)258-2633		X	X	#	#
Collette Tours, 162 Middle Street, Pawtucket, RI 02860, (800)832-4656; (800)752-2655 in New England	X	X	*		*
Escapade Tours, 2200 Fletcher Avenue, Fort Lee, NJ 07024, (800)356-2405	X	X	X	**	**
General Tours, 139 Main Street, Cambridge, MA 02142, (800)221-2216	X	X	X	**	**
Isram Travel, 630 Third Avenue, New York, NY 10017, (800)223-7460	X		X	X	
Kampas International, 2826 East Commercial Blvd., Ft. Lauderdale, FL 33308, (800)233-6422	X	X	X	X	X

Tour Operators and Types of Tours They Offer (Continued)

Tour Operators	Escorted	Independent	Stay-Put	Special Interest	Adventure
Legend Tours, 3990 Old Town Avenue, Suite 100C, San Diego, CA 92110, (800)333-6114	X	X	X		X
Littoral Tours, 615 Hope Road, Bldg. 2, Suite 8B, Eatontown, NJ 07724, (800)346-0212	X	X	X	X	X
Lynott Tours, 350 Fifth Avenue, Suite 2619, New York, NY 10118, (212)760-0101 in New York State; (800)221-2474 elsewhere in the United States	X	X	X	**	X
Meier's World Travel, 6033 W. Century Boulevard, Suite 1080, Los Angeles, CA 90045, (800)937-0700	X		*		
Thomas Cook, 100 Cambridge Park Drive, Cambridge, MA 02140, (617)354-5060 (no 800-number, call local office)	X	X	X	X	X
Thompson Travel Center, 1322 East First Street, Duluth, MN 55805, (800)247-0721	X	X	X	X	X
Trafalgar, 11 East 26th Street, Suite 1300, New York, NY 10010, (800)854-0103	X	X	X		
Travel Bound, 599 Broadway, New York, NY 10012, (800)456-8656	**	X	X	**	**
TWA Getaway Tours, 10 E. Stow Road, Marlton, NJ 08053, (800)GETAWAY	X	X	X		
Unitours, 8 S. Michigan Avenue, Chicago, IL 60603, (800)621-0557 or (312)782-1590	X	X	X	**	
Value Holidays, 10224 N. Port Washington Road, Mequon, WI 53092, (800)558-6850	X	X	X	*	*

Note: Inclusion in this list does not imply an endorsement by the authors or publisher.
Key: * limited; ** customized for groups of 20+ only; # side-trips for additional fee

CHAPTER **2**

TRANSPORTATION OPTIONS

Philip and Joe work for the same import/export company, and were making their plans to attend an annual trade show in London during the off-peak travel season. In an attempt to tighten its corporate belt, their company discontinued its perk of providing business class seats for overseas travel, requiring coach class instead. Philip took the news without much upset. Joe, on the other hand, was so angry he decided to pay for an upgrade and sit in business class. After sitting through dinner and a movie he'd seen before, Joe attempted to get a little rest, but was interrupted by other passengers in the packed business class section. Deciding to stretch his legs instead, Joe strolled back to the near-empty coach section of the plane. As he walked back into coach, Joe noticed Philip, sprawled out across three seats with a pillow and blanket, getting a few hours of sleep before they landed at Heathrow Airport.

What Joe wouldn't have given for a few hours sleep before his plane landed at Heathrow. But because he paid for an upgrade, the bleary-eyed Joe stuck it out in business class and paid for a lack of sleep the entire next day. As for Philip, he knows that sometimes the less desirable deal can turn out to be best after all.

AIR TRAVEL

The first leg of your journey overseas typically includes air travel, with 90 percent of all travel abroad commencing this way. Here are a few insider tips you can follow to ensure the best air travel arrangements possible:

• Schedule "nonstop" flights whenever possible, especially if you are traveling with infants or small children. "Direct" flights typically can include multiple take-offs and landings, which cause more hassles and problems for those with sensitive ears. And if you must use "connecting" flights, try to avoid airports known for their congestion, like John F. Kennedy in New York or O'Hare in Chicago. If you're running late for a connecting flight and run into a mob scene, you may not make it.

• Charge your ticket on a credit card, which provides certain protection under federal credit regulations if your airline happens to go bankrupt. You may also receive frequent flyer miles if you're using a credit card that assigns points for such charges.

And if your ticket is nonrefundable, don't assume that you will lose all the money you paid for the ticket if you don't end up taking the trip. Often, an airline will apply the amount you paid as a credit, and you can use this credit to buy another ticket within the next year in most cases.

• Check recent history for previous terrorist events to avoid traveling to certain destinations on anniversary dates of previous incidents.

• Check fares until the day you depart, even after you have purchased your ticket. If your fare is reduced, the airline may refund the difference, but *you* have to ask for it.

• Confirm your flight and its departure time a day or two before you're scheduled to fly. The airline can change the flight time without notifying you. When you confirm, provide a phone number where you can be reached in case the flight is canceled at the last minute.

• Arrive at the airport early. Often airlines will ask you to be there two hours before an international flight is scheduled to leave. If you're the last one there, you could lose your seat, due to overbooking.

• Check your airline's baggage restrictions before you pack. Most airlines allow travelers departing from the United States to carry on one bag (weighing less than 50 pounds) and to check two bags, each totaling 62 linear inches (length, width, and depth added together) and weighing less than 70 pounds each. Additional bags may be surcharged, so ask your travel agent or the airline about the restrictions on luggage for your specific destination. For more information on luggage, see Chapter 12.

• Ask your travel agent or airline about airport departure taxes you might encounter during your trip, and designate a portion of your budget to cover such costs.

• Check into your "rights" as an air traveler, including such areas as delayed and canceled flights, overbooking, lost and damaged luggage, airline safety, and air fares. These publications can help:

Fly Rights (prepared by the U.S. Department of Transportation), Consumer Information Center, P.O. Box 100, Pueblo, CO 81002 (cost is $1).

Facts & Advice for Airline Passengers, the Aviation Consumer Action Project, P.O. Box 19029, Washington, DC 20036 (cost is $5).

Plane Talk, a series of fact sheets covering "Tips for Defensive Flying," "Public Charter Flights," "Transporting Live Animals," "The Disabled Traveler," and "Tips on Avoiding Baggage Problems." For free copies, write the Office of Consumer Affairs, U.S. Department of Transportation, I-25, Washington, DC 20590.

How to Save Money on Air Travel.   Rely on a trusted travel agent to find you the best airfare. Since agents are compensated by carriers—not travelers—you have the freedom to choose the very best available to you. Their knowledge of travel will help you secure the best rate.

Airfares for traveling overseas change—often dramatically within a given season. Usually it's cheaper to fly to Europe in the fall and winter. While a winter trip may not offer as much sun and warm breezes, ask anyone who's been to Venice when they prefer to go. Chances are, they prefer the grey winter skies mixed with the vibrant colors of buildings to the Venice of summer, when the smells from the canals can be overwhelming. So, if cost is an issue, travel "off season."

Check into frequent flyer programs; they have made travel abroad more affordable. Many people who travel frequently on business accumulate mileage points and use them for vacation travel.

Remember, airlines aren't the only travel service providers awarding frequent flyer miles. Now, you can earn frequent flyer points from credit card companies, hotels, and even long-distance telephone companies. Citibank, for example, offers a credit card that accumulates points toward American Airlines' AAdvantage program. MCI, the long-distance telephone company, assigns points usable on American's and Northwest's programs. Many hotels are in on the act, too.

TRAVEL TIP   To maximize your participation in frequent flyer programs, consider purchasing *The Official Frequent Flyer Guidebook* by Randy Peterson (AirPress, 4715-C Town Center Drive, Colorado Springs, CO 80916, (719)597-8889). The book offers tips on a range of airline, hotel, car rental, and credit card programs. ■

The New Euro Flyer Pass.   If you're planning to fly to one destination in Europe and then to several other cities before returning to the United States, consider the Euro Flyer Pass. Four European airlines have joined to offer this service, which extends to more than 100 destinations in Europe.

The pass is good for use on the European routes of Air France (and its subsidiary, Air Inter), Czechoslovak Airlines, and Sabena. Passengers buy between three and nine coupons, each costing $120. Each coupon is good for a one-way trip between two European cities.

Travelers must buy the coupon book in the United States when purchasing their tickets to Europe, with round-trip travel to the original destination city required. The result is a savings of more than half of what you would pay for the tickets once you're in Europe. Prices for children are even lower.

For more information on the Euro Flyer Pass, call Air France at (800)237-2747, Czechoslovak Airlines at (212)682-5833, or Sabena at (800)955-2000.

SELECTING YOUR SEAT ON AN AIRPLANE

TIP #1: When making airline reservations, try to obtain a pre-assigned seat. If you cannot obtain a pre-assigned seat on the day you purchase your tickets, there are two other options:

1. Keep asking your travel agent to try to book a specific seat. Often, a few days before the flight, the airlines will open up the "seating map" and allow seating assignments.

Middle seats on crowded airplanes can mean hours of torture, so select your seat carefully.

2. If you happen to be in an airport on an intervening trip, stop by the airline counter to ask about assigning a seat for the up-coming flight.

If you have preferences in seating (aisle vs. window or front of the plane vs. back), it's a good idea to leave those specific instructions with your travel agent as a standing request.

TIP #2:   Select a seat based on your personality and personal needs.

Passengers who choose seats toward the rear of the aircraft are permitted to board before passengers seated in the front, but after those with children or people who may need special assistance. That means you'll have first crack at spaces in the overhead compartments—often a potential problem on crowded flights. Also, seats near the rear usually are closer to the bathroom facilities.

Passengers who select seats in the front of the plane are the last to board. But sitting in the front means there is a minimum wait to disembark. So, if you're in a hurry to deplane, or are just plain impatient, sit in the front. Finally, those seated in the front are usually the first to be served refreshments and meals.

Aisle seats offer quick access and exit without disturbing others in your row. Yet, you may dislike having other passengers and crew members constantly passing in the aisle, brushing up against your arm or shoulder—maybe even tripping over your foot!

Window seats provide a view and a side of the cabin's interior wall to rest your head against when sleeping. Also, you are never disturbed by people entering or exiting your row—yet, it is troublesome to bother them when you want to get out.

Some additional considerations in selecting an airplane seat include:

• Check with airline gate agents before boarding to see if other cabins within your aircraft are less crowded. Upgrading or downgrading your ticket accordingly may provide you with less cramped quarters, space to stretch out, and an opportunity to grab forty winks during the flight.

• If your assigned seat number is very low, it may be a bulk-head seat. (Bulkhead refers to that single line of seats immediately behind the partition, or bulkhead, that separates either the cockpit, the galley or the first-class section from the aircraft's other cabins.) Some travelers prefer bulkhead seats, since all the distractions are behind them. However, bulkhead seats offer limited area to store carry-on luggage.

• Inquire at the gate to see if your seat is in the emergency exit row. This has two advantages: safety (it's the quickest exit in case of an emergency) and extra leg room (such rows are deeper than others). However, sitting in emergency exit rows requires accepting responsibility for being physically capable of standing and removing the exit hatch, if need be.

• Be sure your seat reclines. On many aircraft, the row of seats ahead of emergency exits do not recline. When your seat does not recline, it can mean an uncomfortable ride, especially if the flight is lengthy or you suffer from back problems.

TIP #3:   Keep your wits about you as you travel to your seat. For instance, glance ahead to look for empty space in an overhead compartment near your seat. It's wise to keep your carry-on luggage as close to your seat as possible. Reach up and grab a pillow, and perhaps a blanket as well, from the open overhead compartments. They often go fast once people are aboard. A pillow or blanket can double as a headrest or lap rest for books and papers.

Check and recheck your seat assignment as you settle in. There's nothing worse than settling into a seat and unpacking your magazines, only to be kicked out by the person who should be sitting there instead. Keep your boarding pass handy to show any other passenger or flight attendant who might challenge your seat assignment.

TIP #4:   If your business budget permits, consider flying first class. You can make excellent business contacts. Yes, it is more expensive, but you'll find that *many first-class travelers are senior executives* and, more often than not, they are interesting people and good conversationalists . . . that is, if they are disposed to conversation. You'd be amazed at how many useful business connections are made in first-class seats on long flights.

For example, Jim Fitzgerald, owner of the Golden State Warriors basketball team, tells of one occasion many years ago when he struck up a conversation with a fellow passenger in first class. As a result, he hired the man to help him invest in a then embryonic business called cable television!

CRUISING THE HIGH SEAS

They say "what goes around, comes around." Such is the case with cruising, which at one time was the only way to travel overseas. Today, travelers are revisiting this tradition by heading overseas—Europe especially—on cruise packages.

Even more popular as a travel option is cruising *around* Europe. Such intra-European cruises allow day trips into popular cities, with all the luxury and entertainment of a four-star hotel.

Advantages of Cruises

- Simpler travel expense planning: Total price covers room, food, and entertainment (alcoholic beverages are usually extra).
- Inclusion of air travel to the ship, which can cost considerably less since airline tickets are part of a "package."
- Generous discounts, especially if planning and booking occurs four to six months before departure.
- Minimized currency fluctuation problems, since you pay the entire cost in U.S. dollars up front. When you travel overseas, the currency fluctuates daily and the cost of your room and food can increase (or decrease) on a daily basis.

Disadvantages of Cruises

- Feeling confined after being on a ship for a week or more—especially if you had to settle for less expensive, cramped accommodations.
- Formal attire, especially in the evenings. If dressing formally turns you off, consider other options.
- Limited time to explore the sights on land. Cruise ships usually dock for short periods of time. You won't get to experience a city as much as you would by staying there for several days or a week.
- Seasickness.

Staterooms on cruise ships often provide limited space, so find out what you're getting when making reservations.

Selecting a Cruise. In selecting a cruise, you must be specific about where you want to go (the options are mind-boggling), how long you want to be gone, how much you can afford to spend, and the type of experience you want to have. This last point is especially important because different cruise lines offer different experiences, from *tres chic* to economy.

Accommodations on cruise ships—typically called staterooms—can vary in size, appointments, and price. Outside staterooms will cost more, since they provide a view through a porthole. But be careful in letting a travel agent sell you a fancy stateroom with a fabulous view: With all the distractions and attractions of a cruise ship, you'll undoubtedly spend little time in your room.

While a travel agent can be very helpful in charting a course for you, it's not unusual for travelers to book such trips directly with cruise lines. The following list includes a few you can contact:

Carnival	(800)327-9501
Club Med	(800)CLUB-MED
Crystal Cruises	(800)446-6645
Cunard	(800)221-4770
Diamond Cruise	(800)333-3333
Princess Cruises	(800)421-0522
Royal Caribbean Cruise Line	(800)432-6559
Royal Cruise Line	(800)792-2992
Royal Viking Line	(800)422-8000
Seabourn Cruise Line	(800)929-9595

For the uninitiated, it may be best to work with a "cruise only" travel agency, rather than your usual agency. Such firms can provide an orientation to the art of cruising, as well as myriad details about what will go on. For a list of cruise only agencies, contact the National Association of Cruise Only Agencies at P.O. Box 7209, Freeport, NY 11520, (516)378-8006.

To learn more about cruising on your own, contact the Cruise Line International Association for their free brochure, *Cruising: Answers to Your Questions,* at 500 Fifth Avenue, Suite 1407, New York, NY 10111, (212)921-0066.

When making your cruise preparations, ask your travel agent or cruise line representative about:

- *Dress codes.* Be sure you're prepared for all occasions, including the one or more formal attire evenings usually included during a cruise itinerary.
- *Sports activities.* Both on board and in ports (if you're a tennis, golf, or jogging enthusiast, there's a cruise for you!).
- *Gratuities.* Typically not built into the all-inclusive cruise price, you don't want to be short of currency for tips to your cabin steward, waiter, or dining room maitre'd (all of whom *expect* a

tip as part of cruising's culture). While most ships provide printed guidelines upon boarding about when, how much, and whom to tip, it is wise to request this information from your travel agent or cruise line prior to your departure.

TRAVEL TIP Just as you would not pack your passport, never place your cruise documentation in checked luggage—you'll need this paperwork in order to board the ship. ■

RIDING THE RAIL

Once you've hit the ground, one of the most popular, economical, and restful ways to see a foreign country is by rail. In Europe especially, train travel can be very efficient, since cities are close enough together and easily accessible by train.

Rail passes are available through travel agents, and offer the advantage of unlimited train travel and, frequently, connections with other modes of ground transportation. But travelers usually must purchase rail passes—especially the Eurailpass or Britrail pass (for England, Scotland, and Wales)—*before they leave the United States*. Eurailpasses, the original and still most popular of all rail passes, can be purchased in many variations from Rail Europe, the North American sales agent for most European railroads. A flat fee allows travel all over the continent for a specific time limit. Or, travelers can pay just to travel in one country. Either can include sleeping accommodations.

Valid in Austria, Belgium, Denmark, Finland, France, Germany, Greece, Holland, Hungary, Ireland, Italy, Luxembourg, Norway, Portugal, Spain, Sweden, and Switzerland, Eurailpasses allow you to travel in first-class accommodations, unless you've purchased the Youthpass (for those under age 26), which is good for second-class travel only. Most passes also include free or discounted travel on steamers, ferries, and national bus lines.

For more information, ask your travel agent or send for a free *Rail Europe Traveler's Guide,* P.O. Box 10383, Stamford, CT 06904, (800)4-EURAIL or (800)438-7245.

TRAVEL TIP Do not purchase a Eurailpass if you want to take a train to one location and stay there. Conventional train passes work better, even though you probably won't be able to buy them before you leave home. ■

Special train experiences also exist for travelers who enjoy such trips. The most famous is the Orient Express, the Paris-to-Istanbul extravaganza that was the preferred transportation option for the upper class and nobility of the 1920s. Operating today as the Venice Simplon-Orient Express, the train carries tourists from London to Venice (with stops along the way) twice weekly. For more information, contact Venice Simplon-Orient Express, c/o Abercrombie & Kent, 1520 Kensington Rd., Oak Brook, IL 60521, (800)524-2420. Or, ask your travel agent about this and other train travel experiences.

TRAVEL TIP If you're traveling to Estonia, Latvia, or Lithuania, you can purchase a Baltic Rail Card, which is good for unlimited train travel throughout the three Baltic republics. You can obtain a pass for $50 (for eight days) or $100 (for 15 days), with a $15 handling fee for each card bought in the United States. They're available from Eurocruises and Uniontours in New York, or at railway offices in Finland, Norway, and Sweden. The passes are also good for free re-served sleeping accommodations and discounts on some Baltic ferries and on connecting routes to the Baltic Republics from Sweden, Norway, Finland, eastern portions of Germany, and parts of Poland. For information, call Eurocruises, (800)688-3876 or (212)691-2099; or Uniontours (800)451-9511 or (212)683-9500. Or, contact your travel agent. ■

Modern train service is chancy in most of Latin America and much of Asia. Japan is one exception, offering efficient train travel. Check with your travel agent to be sure.

Tips for Train Travel

- Does your ticket indicate a seat assignment? For Eurail, some special trains require seat reservations and you'll pay a small fee. In most European train stations, you must buy your ticket at one window and then confirm your reservation at another.
- Secure a timetable before you leave home, if possible, and plan your itinerary accordingly. (*Note:* Train timetables are typically published in military time. For instance, a train at 3:00 P.M. would be listed in a train schedule as 15:00.)
- Be sure you're sitting in the car headed for your destination. It's usually indicated on a signboard on the side of the car. Individual cars on European trains often are uncoupled from one train and attached to another headed for a different destination.
- Keep your ticket handy once it's been stamped by the train's conductor. You may need it to disembark.
- Learn pronunciations of your stops before you board, so you'll recognize them when they're called out.

- Bring an extra sweater or jacket, since most trains are drafty.
- Before you leave, check to see if the train includes a dining car. If it doesn't, plan ahead and pack meals to carry on the train with you.
- Carry your own towels, soap, and toilet tissue. Some trains are low on basic supplies.

DRIVING ON YOUR OWN

Driving the cities and countryside of your destination is a flexible way to go, for sure. Unencumbered by scheduled departures and arrivals, you can take in the sights at your leisure.

Road maps are generally readable, but getting behind the wheel in a foreign country requires a fair amount of courage. If possible, before making your decision, spend time talking to someone who has driven the roads of your destination. Inquire about conditions, roadside services, language barriers, and other potential problems. If you can't have such a conversation, then borrow a book from your local library that provides the pertinent details.

Automobile associations and tourist information offices can be another good source of this information, as well as maps that help you plan your route before you ever leave home. A complete listing of tourist information offices in the United States can be found in Appendix B.

TRAVEL TIP Driving in Asia can be particularly challenging. Driving on the left combined with relentless traffic jams may drive you nowhere but crazy. ■

Renting a Car.   The best way to rent a car overseas is to book it before you depart. You can do this through your travel agent (see Chapter 1), or by calling an international car rental company like Avis, Hertz, Dollar Rent-A-Car, Budget, Thrifty Rent-A-Car, or National. Check your phone book for their toll-free reservation numbers. Another option to consider is a fly/drive tour package, which combines air travel and car rental in one deal, but must be arranged before departure.

A new, alternative service that people are using is the U.S.-based wholesale car-rental firm, which can save one-third of the cost of renting a car overseas. Car rental wholesalers, who sometimes double as tour operators, are able to negotiate special rates based on volume discounts they receive from rental companies like Hertz and Avis. But such wholesalers don't advertise to the general public because of fears that everyone will want the wholesale price. You can ask your travel agent about reserving a car through a car-rental wholesaler or tour operator, or, if you're looking to rent a car in Europe, call one of these companies directly:

Auto Europe	(800)223-5555
Connex International	(800)333-3949
DER Tours	(800)937-1234
Meier's World Travel	(800)937-0700
Kemwel Group	(800)678-0678

Car rentals around the world require a valid driver's license, and in some countries, an International Driving Permit (see page 29 for instructions on how to obtain one). You must also present an internationally accepted credit card to rent a car in most countries as a deposit, even if you're paying your bill in cash. Check with your car rental firm to determine which credit cards are accepted in your destination country.

No matter how you reserve your rental car, there are several important questions to ask about the rules of your destination:

- Is there an age minimum or maximum? (Minimums range from 18 to 21 years of age, and in some countries, adults over the age of 60 are not allowed to drive.)
- Are prices guaranteed in U.S. dollars or the foreign currency?
- Is payment in local currency required?
- Is there a penalty for cancellation?
- Is mileage unlimited?
- Is a deposit other than a credit card required?
- Is there a penalty if you drop off the car in a different location from your pick-up? (Some countries in Asia will not allow renters to drive cars over country borders.)
- How much will you be charged for the value-added tax? (It varies by country.)
- How much will you be charged for the collision damage waiver? (Note: Many credit card companies, which previously covered car rental insurance for cardholders, have eliminated this benefit. Check with your credit card issuer and your personal car insurance company to see if you are covered, thus avoiding this costly expense.) Also, read Chapter 11 on insurance for further details regarding auto insurance.
- Do you have to rent the car for a minimum number of days?
- Does the car have automatic transmission and air conditioning? If it does, will that add to your cost?

Long-Term Car Rentals/Leasing.   If you're staying in Europe for three weeks or more, you may want to check into leasing a car. The greatest advantage of such a program is cost, since car rental taxes are typically avoided and collision damage waivers not included. Under these programs, drivers 18 and older receive a brand new car on a short-term lease plan, offering a wide choice of cars and options (like automatic transmissions and air conditioning), and a wide variety of pick-up and drop-off options, some of which are free. For more information about two such programs, contact Renault USA, 650 1st Ave., New York, NY 10016, (800)221-1052 or Peugeot Motors of America, 1 Peugeot Plaza, P.O. Box 607, Lyndhurst, NJ 07071, (201)935-8400. Ask your travel agent about other such programs.

Car Safety.   In any country you visit, you do have to obey their laws and rules. If you're driving, the rules are of the utmost importance, especially in the 51 countries where cars drive on the left side of the road. In these countries, ignoring the rules could not only get you a traffic ticket, it could get you killed.

Each country has it's own rules. For instance, you can be fined $1,000 in Indonesia for running a red light and even more for not wearing a seat belt. In Mexico City, travelers are restricted from driving on certain days. Check with embassies or consulates regarding the driving laws of each country in which you plan to drive.

Street and highway signs are typically easy to read, but pay particular attention to parking signs in larger cities. Unlike the United States, where violating a parking sign results in a ticket, cars illegally parked in overseas cities can be towed, "booted," or sometimes damaged by over zealous parking enforcers. When in doubt, ask someone what a particular sign means.

Obtaining an IDP and Auto Insurance.   If you are a frequent world traveler and you like to drive while you're away, you may want to obtain an International Driving Permit (IDP) or an Inter-American Driving Permit (IADP) for Central and South America. U.S. licenses are honored in Canada, in most Western European countries and the Caribbean, but in other places an IDP is required to drive any vehicle, including a rental car.

Printed in seven languages and good for one year, IDPs cost $10 and are available from any branch of the American Automobile Association, (800)765-4222. You'll need a valid driver's license and two passport-size photos to apply.

When determining *where* an IDP is required, consider where you'll drive—not just where you'll rent. If you will cross borders, you may need an IDP during your journey, even if it's not required in the location where you're renting or returning your vehicle. And should you be stopped by local police, don't assume that they can read your English-language driver's license.

If you travel infrequently and visit countries that cater to English-speaking travelers, you probably won't need an IDP. You may, in fact, get a blank stare from an employee of a rental car agency when you hand him or her one. In this case, just use your U.S. driver's license.

Proof of liability insurance also may be necessary to rent, lease, or purchase a car overseas. An International Insurance Certificate, or Green Card, can be obtained for this purpose from your insurance agent. Some countries, however, can require you to purchase a specific insurance policy from their government upon entering the country. This was the case in the former Soviet Republics, but it's best to check with your travel agent or automobile association just in case.

TRAVEL TIP   If you've ever tried to merge into traffic at the Arc de Triomphe in Paris, you know what we mean when we say, let someone else do your driving . . . like a taxi. If you really do want the experience of driving in another country, do it this way: Enjoy the city where you're staying during the first week, then rent a car on the edge of the city. Pick up a car early on a Saturday or Sunday morning and head out to enjoy the countryside for a week. You'll also find the cost of hotels and food much lower outside the city, especially during the off-season. Come back to the city the following weekend (early on a Saturday morning) and then, if it's time for you to return home, pick a flight leaving Sunday afternoon. That way you're relaxed when returning home, but you still have Saturday afternoon and Sunday morning to enjoy the city before you leave. One more word of advice: It's often a bad idea to return to the city by car on Sunday afternoon or evening. Many residents escape to the countryside on weekends, and they're all coming back in time for work on Monday. Be careful or you'll be caught in a traffic jam. ■

Leaving the Driving to Someone Else.   An alternative to car rental and leasing—especially in large cities where getting around can be complicated and costly, or when traveling between cities and countrysides—is hiring a local car and driver on a daily or weekly basis. Doing so can get you around local driving restrictions, minimize driving problems, and help avoid getting lost. And in the Asian culture, having a car and driver is a protocol issue; certain classes of business persons *never* drive themselves anywhere.

The best way to secure a reliable service is to contact your destination hotel's concierge before you travel. Some travel agents can help, but your best bets are arranged through your hotel.

Airport Limos.   If you're not renting a car, boarding a train, or hopping a cruise ship when you arrive at your destination, and you desire more peace of mind than a local taxicab ride, you may want to pre-arrange for a limousine to meet you.

One service known throughout the world is Carey Limousines. Carey operates in Eastern and Western Europe, Central and South America, Asia and Australia, requiring only 48 hours' notice to book a car and driver. Charges are billed to a major credit card in U.S. dollars *after* service is rendered. To make a reservation or to request their brochure, contact Carey's International Division at (800)336-4646.

Another service, Dav El Chauffeured Transportation Network, also operates in many overseas countries. For reservations, call Dav El's Worldwide Reservation Center at (800)922-0343 or call their National Administration and Sales Office at (800)223-7664 with questions or other inquiries.

CHAPTER **3**

PASSPORTS AND VISAS

Jack, an international marketing consultant from Chicago, was offered the opportunity of a lifetime last year when he was asked to present his firm's credentials for work on a large international sporting event. Required to travel to Europe to make the presentation, Jack quickly telephoned his travel agent to make all the necessary arrangements. Consumed with pulling together his presentation, Jack forgot to check his passport until three days before departure. It had expired. Since it was the middle of February—peak season for passport processing—and Jack couldn't contrive a convincing emergency, neither the government nor his local passport office could help. Finally, after hours of calls and buckets of sweat, Jack found a passport service in Washington, DC, that promised 36-hour turnaround. As it turned out, Jack had to make a connection at Dulles Airport so he could pick up his new passport on his way out of the country.

For many people, Jack's near miss strikes a chord. Those of us who travel abroad frequently have recurring nightmares about renewing, misplacing, or losing a passport. The fact is a passport is absolutely necessary for overseas travel. No passport, and you'll be sightseeing in Newark instead of Nepal.

There are some exceptions. If you're planning a short jaunt to Canada, Mexico, or a Caribbean island, you may not need a passport at all. But even if your trip doesn't require a passport, you're going to have to prove your citizenship to the U.S. Immigration Service before you can come back into the United States.

YOUR PASSPORT: THE BEST PROOF

Your passport permits entry to any foreign country around the world. While documentation requirements vary from country to country, you can count on needing a passport and possibly a visa or tourist card each time you step outside our borders. You also may need evidence that you have enough money for your trip and that you've got ongoing or return transportation tickets. And if you're traveling on business, some countries require a letter of invitation or confirmation before they'll let you in.

TRAVEL TIP If you're planning a trip now and you don't have a passport, apply for one right away. If you have one, check its expira-

32

tion date and apply for renewal if needed. And have your passport application or renewal request completed before you make nonrefundable payments or deposits for travel. If your documentation isn't in order in time for your trip, you could lose prepayments. ■

If your passport is valid for only another six months or less, some countries won't let you in. And if your passport expires while you're traveling, it will cost you a $100 waiver fee to get back into the United States.

APPLYING FOR A PASSPORT

Every year, the flood of passport applications begins in January and slows to a mere trickle by August. That means you can expedite processing of your passport by applying between September and December. That doesn't guarantee you'll get your passport quickly, but it increases your odds.

TRAVEL TIP   Apply early and allow at least six weeks to get your passport—more if you apply during the first half of the year. You can cut your processing time if you apply in person at a passport office. ■

Some countries demand visas to cross their borders, and it will take you about two weeks to obtain each visa you need. Since *you need a completed passport to obtain visas,* the importance of securing your passport early increases.

For your first passport, *you must appear in person* with a completed Form DSP-11, Passport Application, at one of 13 U.S. passport agencies or at any of the thousands of federal or state courthouses or post offices authorized to accept passport applications. To find the addresses of facilities in your area, look in the government listings of your telephone book. You must also apply in person if your last passport expired more than 12 years previously, or if you were formerly included on a family member's passport.

What You Need to Apply for Your First Passport.   When you show up, you need to have:

1. A properly completed, but unsigned, passport application. *Don't sign it!*

2. Proof of citizenship (one of the following):

• If you were born in the United States, a *certified* copy of your birth certificate (which includes the registrar's signature and a seal). If you can't get your birth certificate, submit a notice from a state registrar stating that no birth record exists, accompanied by the best secondary evidence possible (baptismal certificate, hospital birth record, affidavits of people with knowledge of the facts of your birth, or documentary evidence like an early census, school records, family Bible records or newspaper files). A personal-knowledge affidavit should be supported by at least one public record reflecting birth in the United States.

• If you were born outside the United States, you can use a certificate of naturalization, a certificate of citizenship, a report of Birth Abroad of a Citizen of the United States of America (Form FS-240), or a certification of Birth (Form FS-545 or SD-1350).

If you don't have any of these documents and you are a U.S. citizen, take all available proof of citizenship to the nearest U.S. passport agency and ask for help in proving your citizenship.

3. A previous U.S. passport (see above conditions), a certificate of naturalization or citizenship, a valid driver's license, or a government (federal, state, municipal) identification card to establish your identity to the satisfaction of the person accepting your application. If you can't present one of these, you must be accompanied by a U.S. citizen or a permanent resident of the United States who has known you for at least two years. That person will have to establish his or her own identity, must sign an affidavit in the presence of the official who executes the passport application, and you'll have to submit some identification. (A Social Security card, a learner's permit or temporary driver's license, a credit card, any temporary or expired ID card, or any document that has been altered or changed in any way *cannot* be used to establish identity.) If you have no documents, no friends, and amnesia, you're out of luck!

4. Two identical photos of yourself taken within the past six months. They shouldn't be larger than 2 by 2 inches, in either black-and-white or color, and show only your full face on a white background. Don't use photos that are retouched, or from vending machines. Have them taken at a passport photo studio, many of which are located within walking distance of passport offices or federal buildings.

TRAVEL TIP Get extra sets of your passport photos for visa applications and your international driver's permit. Keep an extra with you during travel in case your passport is lost or stolen and you must replace it. ∎

5. The correct fee. Applicants age 18 or over who must appear in person have to pay $65 for their passport (which includes a $10 execution fee). The passport is valid for 10 years. Applicants under 18 pay $40, and the passport is valid for five years. You can pay by check, bank draft, or money order. You can also pay cash at passport agencies and some—but not all—post offices and clerks of court.

Passport Renewal. If you're renewing an expired passport, submit it with your application. If you can't, you'll be asked to provide the original passport number and issue date. If your passport is lost or stolen, you'll have to fill out—*Surprise!*—Form DSP-64, "Statement Regarding Lost or Stolen Passport," along with a new application.

Applying by Mail. You can apply for a passport by mail if *all* the following are true:

- You've been issued a passport within 12 years of your renewal application;
- You submit your most recent U.S. passport with your new application;
- Your previous passport was issued on or after your 16th birthday; and
- Your name is the same as that on your most recent passport (or you've had it changed by marriage or court order).

To apply by mail, get Form DSP-82, "Application for Passport by Mail," from one of the offices accepting applications or from your travel agent, and complete the information requested on the reverse side of the form.

1. Sign and date the application.
2. Include your departure date. (It will help speed the process.)
3. Enclose your previous passport.
4. Enclose two identical 2 by 2-inch regulation passport photos.
5. Enclose the $55 passport fee. (The $10 execution fee is not required if you apply by mail.) You can pay with a personal check, a bank draft or cashier's check, or a money order. *Don't send cash through the mail!*
6. If you've changed your name, submit the original or certified copy of the court order or marriage certificate that shows the name change.

For processing, mail the completed application and attachments to one of the passport agencies. *An incomplete or improperly prepared application will delay issuance of your passport*—and you'll probably have to fill out even more forms.

Send your completed Form DSP-82 and accompanying enclosures to the Passport Lockbox, P.O. Box 371971, Pittsburgh, PA 15250. Direct any questions or inquiries to the National Passport Center, 31 Rochester Avenue, Portsmouth, NH 03801. And, if you're concerned about receiving your passport in time for your departure, consider using overnight mail or courier for your application, and enclose a return self-addressed stamped envelope for your processed passport.

Your previous passport and the original documents you've submitted will be returned to you with your new passport.

TRAVEL TIP When you receive your passport, sign it right away! Then fill in page 4, Personal Notification Data. ■

PASSPORTS FOR CHILDREN

Applicants between ages 13 and 18 must appear in person with a parent or legal guardian. For kids under 13, a parent or legal guardian may appear on their behalf.

Check with embassies or consulates in the countries you plan to visit about the documents needed for children traveling alone or with one parent. Some countries—especially in Latin America—require single parents to present certified divorce decrees, the deceased parent's death certificate, or written, translated, and notarized permission from the absent parent.

HOW TO GET A PASSPORT IN AN EMERGENCY

Passport agencies can issue a passport quickly when there's a genuine, documented emergency. If you're leaving within five days and need a passport, you can have it delivered by express mail (if you arrange and pay for it in advance). Check with the post office or courthouse that accepts your application, or with the nearest passport agency for specific details.

For a fee, there are companies that will take completed, endorsed passport and visa applications to the Washington, DC, passport office and embassies. Their employees will stand in lines, navigate the bureaucracies, and pick up completed documents for you. They'll run your interference and they'll arrange letters of invitation for countries that require them.

These companies turn around your passport or visa depending on what you're willing to pay. In emergencies, they can even get passports and visas in a single business day. For obvious reasons, these companies are all located in and around our nation's capitol. They include:

A Travisa
2122 P Street, N.W.
Washington, DC 20037
(202)463-6166

All Points Visa, Inc.
4900 Auburn Avenue, Suite 201
Bethesda, MD 20814
(301)652-9055

Ambassador Visa
2025 I Street, N.W., Suite 806
Washington, DC 20006
(202)728-6701

Atlas Visa Services
2341 Jefferson Davis Highway
Arlington, VA 22202
(703)521-6400

Center for International Business
and Travel
2135 Wisconsin Avenue, N.W.,
Suite 400
Washington, DC 20007
(202)333-5550

DMS Visa International
1611 Connecticut Avenue, N.W.,
Suite 1
Washington, DC 20009
(202)745-3815

Deran Visa Service
1701 Wind Haven Way
Vienna, VA 22180
(703)281-4743

Duke's Visa Service
2033-A 38th Street, S.E.
Washington, DC 20020
(202)583-0280

Embassy Visa Service
2162 California Street, N.W.
Washington, DC 20008
(202)387-1171

Express Visa Service
2150 Wisconsin Avenue, N.W.
Washington, DC 20007
(202)337-2442

Globetrotters
935 South Buchanan Street
Arlington, VA 22204
(703)533-2999

Nader Visa Service, Inc.
1325 18th Street, N.W.
Washington, DC 20036
(202)332-7797

Visa Advisors
1808 Swann Street, N.W.
Washington, DC 20009
(202)797-7976

Wakay Visa Services, Inc.
1519 Connecticut Avenue, N.W.
Washington, DC 20036
(202)337-0300

Washington Visa and Travel
Document Center
2025 I Street, N.W.
Washington, DC 20006

Zierer Visa Service
1521 New Hampshire Avenue,
N.W., Suite 100
Washington, DC 20036
(202)265-3007

TRAVEL TIP   If you travel abroad frequently, or stay for long periods of time, ask your relatives or associates in the United States to keep valid passports. That way, should you become seriously ill or involved in some other emergency, they can travel without delay. ■

AMENDING YOUR PASSPORT

Passports should be amended under the following conditions to remain valid:

- To show a name change.
- To correct descriptive data (address, occupation, business phone, death of a spouse).
- To add visa pages.
- To extend the validity of a limited passport.
- To show endorsement or validation of your passport, if needed.

To apply to amend and validate your passport, complete, sign, and date the passport amendment/validation application. Send it with your passport and any required additional evidence required to make the change to the nearest passport office. *You don't have to appear in person, and there's no fee.* Your amended/validated passport and any evidence you submit will be returned to you.

Altering your U.S. passport in any way (other than changing the personal notification data) is against the law.

WHAT TO DO IF YOUR PASSPORT IS LOST OR STOLEN

If such a fate befalls you before you travel, report a lost or stolen passport immediately to Passport Services, 1425 K Street N.W., Department of State, Washington, DC 20524, (202)647-0518, or to the nearest passport agency.

If your passport is lost or stolen while you're traveling, report the loss immediately to the local police and to the nearest U.S. embassy or consulate. You'll get a new passport much faster if you can provide the consulate with the information that's in it.

TRAVEL TIP   Photocopy the data page of your passport along with other important travel documents and keep them in a separate place. In addition, leave the passport number, date, and place it was issued with a friend or relative in the United States. And take extra passport photos and proof of your American citizenship with you. That way, you'll make it easier to replace a lost passport. You will be asked, though, to pay the normal processing fees. ■

Copy, copy, copy your valuable travel documents *before* you go.

HOW TO PROTECT YOUR PASSPORT

Guard your passport carefully. It is your most valuable travel document because it confirms your U.S. citizenship. In some countries, you'll need it when you pick up mail and check into hotels, embassies, or consulates. As a result, it's a real prize for pickpockets and thieves.

TRAVEL TIP If you have an expired passport, throw it in the bottom of your luggage. Should the original become lost or stolen while traveling, take the old passport to any U.S. embassy or consulate, where they should be able to issue you a new one quickly. ■

- To foil pickpockets, carry photocopies of your passport while you're sightseeing. Leave the original in the hotel safe, not in your empty hotel room or packed in your luggage. If you're traveling with family, make each person responsible for his or her own passport, rather than having one person carry them all.
- When you must carry your passport, hide it securely on your person. Keep it in a security pouch under your clothing, or a zippered or buttoned pocket. Be extra careful in large crowds.
- You do need to have your passport available when you fly. In some countries, you may be asked to fill out a police card listing your name, passport number, destination, local address, and reason for traveling.

• Don't worry if you are asked to leave your passport at the hotel reception desk overnight so it may be checked by local police officials. In some places, local laws dictate these procedures. But if your passport is not returned to you the following morning, report it immediately to local police and the nearest U.S. embassy or consulate.

OBTAINING VISAS

A visa is an endorsement or stamp placed in your passport by a foreign government that permits you to visit that country for a specified purpose and period of time—say, a three-month tourist visa.

Many countries—especially in Africa, Asia, and the South Pacific, and some in Latin America—require that travelers from the United States get visas before they come. This process can take two weeks, so plan accordingly. To apply for a visa, you'll have to:

• Submit a valid U.S. passport;
• Complete an application form;
• Supply passport-type photos;
• Pay a fee; and
• Submit the documents in person or by mail to the country's embassy in Washington, DC, or to its nearest consulate office.

It's important to find out the exact requirements of each country you plan to visit. You'd hate to be turned away at the border because you didn't get a visa.

For specific entry requirements of every country, and information on how to apply for visas and tourist cards, get a copy of the State Department's *Foreign Entry Requirements* publication. You can order it for 50¢ from the Consumer Information Center, Pueblo, CO 81009. It's updated every year, but may not reflect the most current requirements.

TRAVEL TIP To be absolutely up-to-date on current entry requirements, contact the embassy or consulate of each country you plan to visit. ■

Some Middle Eastern countries won't let you in if your passport has been stamped by Israel, while others do not allow entry to travelers bearing South African visas. Some countries require letters of invitation (from host companies if you're traveling on business; from a travel agency or reserved hotel if you're a tourist). And some countries require an official letter from the host government allowing you to come before they'll issue you a visa. Bottom line: Check the details.

Since visas are stamped directly onto a blank page of your passport, you need to give your passport to an official of each foreign embassy or consulate. You'll also need to fill out a form, and you may need one or more photos. Many visas also require a fee.

There are two types of visas—tourist and business. If you travel often to one country on a tourist visa, officials might suspect you're trying to avoid taxes. To avoid such problems, make sure you have the right visa. And if you plan to stay in one country for a long time, some countries offer long-term visas (for an additional fee). Check with the embassy or consulate to find out.

Also check with embassies, consulates or tourist information offices about vaccinations, exit requirements, and any travel restrictions for tourists.

TRAVEL TIP If you need additional visa pages before your passport expires, submit it to a local passport agency. If you travel frequently to countries that require visas, you can get a 48-page passport at no additional charge. ■

Other special visa circumstances include cruises (upon docking, government officials board incoming ships for entry documentation that cruise personnel prepare on your behalf) and trains (in some countries government officials will board trains during regularly scheduled stops and expect *all* passengers to have entry visas—even those passengers not exiting the train in that country). Check with your travel agent about special circumstances that you may encounter during your trip.

TOURIST CARDS

Some countries require only a tourist card instead of a passport. You can get one from the country's embassy or consulate, from an airline that serves the country, or at the port of entry. As with visas, there can be a fee for tourist cards.

Remember, even if a country doesn't require a passport, it will require some proof of citizenship and identity. And no matter what various countries require, you'll need to prove your identity to get back *into* the United States.

CHAPTER 4

SELECTING THE RIGHT
ACCOMMODATIONS

Katherine's trip to London was off to a great start. Her plane landed on time, without any lost or damaged luggage, and her driver met her at the gate. Upon arriving at her hotel—"a quaint place" recommended by a British friend—she was greeted by a smiling front-desk clerk who promptly found her reservation for a first-class room. Glancing around the lobby, she observed the elegant furniture, wall coverings, and rugs and remembered that her friend had told her the hotel was originally built by King Edward VII in the nineteenth century for his mistress Lillie Langtry. An elevator ride to the seventh floor left Katherine two floors shy of her ninth floor room, accessible only by climbing the stairs. Her room, at the end of the ninth-floor corridor, contained a small bed (covered by a moth-eaten bedspread), a chest of drawers, a bathroom without a toilet, and a tiny window exposing the lower floors' roof. Katherine immediately called the front desk to demand a room change, stating she had requested first-class accommodations. Assuring her that she had received what was requested, the clerk explained that "first class" in London translates to "second class" in America. "This room isn't at all what I expected," Katherine exclaimed. "And if Edward really built this place for Lillie, it's clear you haven't touched it since Lillie moved out!"

Researching lodging options and adjusting your expectations is the first step in selecting accommodations overseas. Just as in the United States, a wide variety of lodging alternatives exists abroad, from standard hotels to inns, bed-and-breakfasts, vacation properties, and hostels. Unfortunately, there are no set international standards. For instance, an overseas hotel rated by a guidebook as four-star might not seem deserving of all four stars. As Katherine discovered, classifications can create confusion: Our definition of "first class" translates into "deluxe" abroad, and "second class" becomes "first class."

There's no need to be suspicious of all lodgings abroad. With proper research and preparation, you should be able to find the right facility to satisfy your tastes, pocketbook, business needs, and personal whims.

Don't be intimidated by a lack of knowledge in such areas. Very few people know that most hotels in India feature "squat" toilets, or that a hotel "garni" in Switzerland serves breakfast and beverages, but no other meals. A few simple steps can get you started:

• Write down what you're looking for. Do you need lodging for just one night, or will you spend enough time in one location so that you can take advantage of your accommodations' amenities? Do you want to savor the countryside and terrain, or do you prefer to be in the heart of a major city? Can your pocketbook handle luxury surroundings, or is economy the way to go?

• Check out a few destination guidebooks. Not only do they list current contact information, but they also provide a brief description of each option's strengths and weaknesses.

• Discuss your findings with a travel agent, who can either confirm your choices or recommend alternatives.

• Consider writing or telephoning the lodging's proprietor to request additional information. Be as specific as you need to be, asking questions about the service, nightlife, size, and general description of bedrooms and public spaces, restaurants, location, and availability of any special services you might require (handicapped facilities, exercise room, children's programs, dietary needs).

Don't be afraid to do your own research and book your accommodations directly. Time zone differences and language barriers may prove troublesome, but if you get started soon enough you'll be successful.

TYPES OF ACCOMMODATIONS

Hotels.   Hotels exist in many sizes and classes of service. However, there are many large U.S.-based and international hotel chains that offer a consistent lodging product around the world. Check your phone book or ask a travel agent for their toll-free reservation numbers.

While European hotels most closely resemble their American counterparts, other parts of the world—especially South America and Asia/Pacific—are quickly catching up. According to industry experts, the nations of Southeast Asia and South America are among the fastest growing visitor markets in the world. As a result, new hotels are cropping up, many owned and operated by such chains as Sheraton, Hilton, Hyatt, Ramada, and Marriott. So don't be afraid that you won't be able to find reasonable accommodations; you may be pleasantly surprised.

Some hotels are privately owned and operated, spanning the gamut from sophisticated five-star resorts to simple cottages in the woods. In dealing with such establishments, remember that you are subject to the standards of comfort and cleanliness set by the property's owner, not a corporation.

One comprehensive source of information about hotels around the world is the *OAG Travel Planner.* Three geographic editions exist:

- *The European Travel Planner Redbook,* which contains information about 35 countries and 12,900 cities throughout Europe;
- *The Business Travel Planner,* which covers the United States, Canada, Mexico, and the island nations of the Caribbean; and
- *The Pacific Asia Travel Planner Redbook,* which details 40 countries from India to Southeast Asia, China, Japan, Malaysia, Australia, and New Zealand.

The books are published every three months and are available from OAG, 2000 Clearwater Drive, Oak Brook, IL 60521, (800)323-3537. Individual quarterly issues are $63 per copy, although annual subscriptions are available for each series for $142.

Hotel Reservation Queries.   When making hotel reservations, either through a travel agent or on your own, ask these questions:

- Does the hotel offer a daily or weekly rate?
- Are discounts available to business travelers, senior citizens, college students, families?
- What are the cancellation provisions; are there penalties for canceling?
- Does the hotel belong to any airline frequent flyer programs? Are there any other perks offered to guests?
- What are check-in and check-out times?
- Can a room be assigned on a low floor, or with a particular view, or near the elevator?
- Is the hotel located near shopping, museums, theaters, beaches, ski slopes, client offices, or other areas of importance to you?
- Does the hotel offer such facilities as a fitness room, swimming pool, tennis courts, sauna, or other recreational areas?

Inns and Bed-and-Breakfasts.   Inns and Bed-and-Breakfasts are an entirely different matter. The atmosphere will generally be less formal, less private, and the ambiance depends entirely on the age (some can be more than 500 years old!) and condition of the facility. Proprietors sometimes offer meals, sometimes not. The more questions you ask in making your plans, the better.

Two good resources for information on bed-and-breakfasts are:

- *The Best Bed & Breakfast in the World,* Worldwide Bed & Breakfast Association, P.O. Box 2070, London W12 8QW, England, (011-4481)742-91-23; and
- Author Karen Brown's series of books published by Globe Pequot, available in most travel book stores.

Vacation Homes. These homes are quickly becoming a popular option, since there are thousands of private homes available for rent in both highly desirable and off-the-beaten-path destinations around the world. This unique form of lodging provides the advantages of a "home away from home" while enabling you to choose your degree of luxury.

Vacation rentals can usually run from $400 per week to over $7,000 plus, depending on location, season, size, and amenities. To further reduce costs, plan your vacation in the off-season, which can knock off as much as 50 percent of the price.

Some of the best bargains can be found through travel companies that list these properties and put you in direct touch with the owner to make your arrangements. One widely accepted resource is the *Worldwide Home Rental Guide,* 369 Montezuma St., Suite 338, Santa Fe, NM 87501, (505)984-2792.

A partial list of companies that offer vacation rental properties around the world follows. If necessary, ask your travel agent for recommendations from this list or other lists of such agencies.

Vacation Rental Property Agencies	*Countries Where Rentals Are Available*
At Home Abroad 405 E. 56th Street, Suite 6H New York, NY 10022 (212)421-9165	Caribbean, England, France, Ireland, Italy, Mexico, Portugal, Spain, West Indies
Interhome 124 Little Falls Road Fairfield, NJ 07004 (201)882-6864	Austria, Belgium, Croatia, Czech Republic, England, Finland, France, Germany, Greece, Italy, Netherlands, Poland, Scotland, Spain, Switzerland, Wales
Rent A Home International 7200 34th Avenue, NW Seattle, WA 98117 (800)488-7368	Austria, Australia, Caribbean, Central America, Cyprus, Denmark, England, France, Germany, Greece, Hungary, Ireland, Italy, Mexico, Netherlands, Portugal, Spain, Switzerland, Turkey

Vacation Rental Property Agencies	*Countries Where Rentals Are Available*
Rent A Vacation (RAVE) 383 Park Avenue Rochester, NY 14607 (716)256-0760	Austria, Caribbean, England, France, Germany, Greece, Ireland, Italy, Mexico, Portugal, Spain, Switzerland, Turkey
Villas International 605 Market Street, Suite 510 San Francisco, CA 94105 (800)221-2260	Austria, Australia, England, France, Germany, Greece, Ireland, Italy, Mexico, Portugal, Scotland, Spain, Switzerland, West Indies

Hostels.   Hostels of various kinds are available for lodging around the world. More than 6,000 locations in over 70 countries offer travelers clean, inexpensive, overnight accommodations. Originally designed for young people traveling on foot or bicycle, this option is ideal for singles of all ages (including senior citizens!) who want to meet others traveling under similar conditions.

The key to hostel success is arriving early in the afternoon, when doors are opened for the evening—to ensure you get a bed. The dormitory-style facilities segregate men and women, although some offer family sleeping rooms that can be reserved in advance. Meals are provided, but toiletries, towels, and bed linens are not. Curfews are often imposed, and advance membership is often required.

Excellent guides to these accommodations are:

- *Hostelling International—Budget Accommodation, Volume I,* covering Europe and the Mediterranean; and
- *Hostelling International—Budget Accommodation, Volume II,* covering the rest of the world.

Each is available for $13.95, which includes postage and handling, from American Youth Hostels, P.O. Box 37613, Washington, DC 20013-7613, (202)783-6161.

OFF THE BEATEN PATH

For a European vacation or business excursion filled with memories, unusual lodgings are definitely worth checking into.

- In *England,* you can choose from an old rectory, manse, or historic estate, where you can become a part of the local landscape without taking on a second mortgage. Review a copy of the *Wolsey Lodges Directory,* available from your travel agent or the British tourist information office.

The Relais et Chateaux organization can provide you with an illustrated catalogue of intimate deluxe havens throughout Europe, ranging from castles and palaces to convents and monasteries. Contact Relais et Chateaux, c/o Mr. Wolfgang Winter, 11 E. 44th St., Suite 707, New York, NY 10017, (212)856-0115.

• In *France,* the Federation Nationale des Gites de France organizes the rentals of gites, which are low-cost country estates, offering a wide range of amenities at varying costs. They are regulated by the French government and available for a week or longer. Contact The French Experience, 370 Lexington Ave., Suite 812, New York, NY 10017, (212)986-1115.

• Gast im Schloss is *Germany*'s association of hotels and restaurants located in castles, mansions, and historic buildings. The prices range from moderate to expensive with information available on facilities in the publication *Gast im Schloss: Castle Hotels,* available from the German tourist information office.

• In *Spain* they call them "paradores"; in *Portugal,* "pousadas." Basically, they're state-run systems of establishments that include castles, convents, palaces, as well as new structures. They offer modern facilities and a wide range of prices. Contact the tourist information office, or ask your travel agent to secure a listing of the properties.

MAKING RESERVATIONS—THE SMART WAY

To get the most for your travel dollar and to confirm that you're getting what you expect, it's wise to make your arrangements several months in advance—especially if you're traveling during peak season.

Travel agents and hotel reps (wholesalers who usually sell to agents, but will also sell direct to travelers) can be especially helpful in making reservations. Well equipped with up-to-the-minute information on discounts, promotional offers and other reservation tricks of the trade, their problem-solving skills can often provide one-stop shopping for all your travel needs.

Another alternative—hotel booking agencies—operate as outlets for underbooked lodgings, but offer the best deals a week or two before departure if you can wait that long. Representing a wide range of properties, a few booking agencies to consider include Hotel Reservations Network, (800)964-6835; Room Exchange, (800)846-7000; Travel Network, (800)477-7172; and Hotels Plus (800)235-0909.

TRAVEL TIP Booking accommodations through a third party typically won't increase your cost. You will normally pay the same price, if not less, as you would if you booked the lodging directly. Such professionals generally offer their services at no charge to the traveler, since they are compensated with commissions from service providers (hotelier, car rental firm, cruise line). There are exceptions: If at your request, an agent books accommodations for you at a lodging that does not pay commissions, you may be charged a fee. ■

When planning your trip, check on rate differences between peak and off-peak seasons for the destinations you've selected. If you can be flexible about dates, scheduling your trip during the off-peak season can save you a considerable amount of money and offer a stay less congested with other tourists.

Most lodgings require deposits (or full prepayment!) before confirming reservations, especially during peak seasons, and some require payment in local currency. (Your travel agent or local banker can help you secure a check in foreign currency, if needed.) Be certain to bring along the receipt from your deposit, whether it be a cash, check, or credit card transaction.

When making reservations, remember that the estimated cost of your accommodations—converted from the local currency into U.S. dollars—can be different when you check in. A stronger dollar at check-in will result in lower cost lodgings; a weaker dollar means you pay more. Ultimately, the proprietor chooses which rate you'll get.

Likewise, the rate you thought you paid with a credit card at check-out can increase or decrease when your bill arrives, depending on when your credit card issuer posts the charge. Your safest bet here is to reserve your lodgings with a credit card, if accepted, then pay with traveler's checks, cash, or a personal check if possible.

Be certain to find out about any local taxes that apply to lodging costs. Also find out beforehand whether the rate for your accommodations includes a service charge, which can sometimes be as much as 20 percent, or whether it will be added at the end of your stay. These taxes and service charges can vary greatly from country to country, and can throw off the entire budget you've prepared for your trip.

And most important of all, make sure you receive a confirmation of your reservation several weeks before you depart. Once received, check it carefully for arrival and departure dates; rate; taxes; applicable deposits, discounts or rebates; cancellation penalties; and other pertinent data.

WHAT IS AND ISN'T INCLUDED?

Estimating your lodging and overall costs for an international trip can be tricky business. Many European lodgings still operate under the pension (*pen-see-yone*) plan. Such plans offer a flat daily or weekly rate, which covers accommodations plus one, two, or all three meals. Find out *what is* and *what isn't* included in your rate before you go. If you don't ask, you could wind up paying for meals twice or being short on the amount you have estimated for meals.

Also, find out what's included in your meals and what's not. Most European hotels offer a continental breakfast consisting of pastries or bread, butter, jam, and

Beware of incidentals that aren't included with your accommodations; otherwise, you could get stuck with *a few* extra charges.

coffee or tea. An American-style breakfast with eggs and bacon will cost you more, unless specified. The same goes for lunch and dinner—extras may be extra. Also be cautious of hotelier and innkeeper invitations: A cordial solicitation to "join us for high tea" could result in charges you weren't counting on when it comes time to check out.

Understanding pension and other plans is important. Basic definitions include:

- *Pension Complete:* Includes continental breakfast, lunch, and dinner.
- *Demi-Pension:* Includes continental breakfast and one other meal, usually dinner.
- *American Plan:* Includes a complete American breakfast, lunch, and dinner.
- *Modified American Plan:* Includes an American breakfast only.

Some hotels and other forms of lodging will provide transfers (bus transportation to and from the airport or train station). Others simply leave it up to you. Check with your travel agent or proprietor beforehand, and make your plans accordingly. If you plan to rent a car, find out if your lodgings offer off-street parking. Many establishments in large cities offer a garage, but charge a flat daily rate.

TRAVEL TIP Beware of voucher programs that cover accommodations, meals, attractions, entertainment, and so on. Most position themselves as "half price or better" deals, but chances are you could have secured such discounts—especially on lodgings—through a travel agent or on your own. Research a voucher program against usual corporate, senior citizen, and other discounts before you buy. ■

CONCIERGE: FRIEND OR FOE?

The term concierge dates back to the Roman Empire, when common slaves stood guard over the doors of inns and dwellings. The concierge was the guard of a castle in the Middle Ages. Today's concierge stands by the principles of Les Clefs d'Or (The Golden Keys), the worldwide professional concierge organization founded in France in 1929.

There is no limit to what a concierge can do to help travelers make up for mishaps, surprises, and inadequate preparation. A good concierge is a vital link to the local environs, providing up-to-date information on sightseeing, transportation, restaurants, entertainment, and other attractions. They can plan family outings, make reservations, access medical assistance and information, baby-sitting services, formalwear rental, and take care of surprises such as flowers, delicacies, and gifts.

A concierge can turn a disaster into sheer delight. Consider Michele and Kevin, who stopped in London on their honeymoon specifically to see *Phantom of the Opera*. In the confusion of wedding and honeymoon preparations, Kevin forgot to reserve tickets, but assumed he could easily pick up two in London. Wrong: The show was sold out for weeks. Michele in tears, Kevin humbly approached the concierge desk with his story.

Later that afternoon, a message was waiting for Kevin and Michele that their tickets could be picked up for the evening performance. Although the price was indecent, Michele and Kevin really didn't care as they watched the performance from their fifth row center seats.

The role of the concierge also can be especially invaluable to business travelers. Faxes, xeroxing, securing clerical assistance, mobile telephones, computer equipment, and translation services should all be available with the assistance of the concierge.

As a result, overseas travelers can leave some local arrangements undone until they arrive, provided their choice of lodging offers concierge service. Check ahead of time—if no assistance will be available, make your local plans before you go.

ARE SPECIAL SERVICES AVAILABLE?

If you have special concerns or requirements from the lodgings you've chosen, it's wise to receive confirmation in writing before your departure that what you require is available.

If handicapped access is necessary during your stay, make certain that you receive detailed information about the accessibility of your accommodations. Although the entrance, elevators, and rooms may be accessible, the dining and entertainment facilities may prove more of a challenge.

Can't leave home without your computer? Overseas wiring is not always compatible with American computer modems. Most hotels owned by U.S. companies have compatible phone jacks, but you could be faced with circuits that jumble your telecommunicated data.

If hotel fire or safety is your concern, be sure your room meets your specific requirements *before* you leave home. (See Chapter 7 for more details on safety.)

PHONING HOME—BARGAIN OR BONANZA?

In-room telephone usage can be a tricky affair in other countries. Because direct-dial phone calls from overseas hotels can be extremely expensive—300 percent to 400 percent added to actual telephone charges in some cases—most American long-distance carriers offer pocket-size cards with access codes to put travelers in touch with U.S. operators at no additional charge. (Beware though, hotels may still charge a "service fee" just for picking up the telephone receiver.)

AT&T's USADirect Service connects callers directly to the United States by dialing an access number, which is always a toll-free or local number. A U.S. operator completes your call, avoiding language barriers and exchange rates. AT&T WorldConnect Service lets travelers make calls between 41 different countries while overseas. Using USADirect access numbers, AT&T operators place calls to any location within WorldConnect countries. All calls are automatically billed to your AT&T Calling Card or another calling card issued by your local telephone company. MCI and Sprint offer similar programs, both direct to the United States and between foreign countries. For more information, contact your long-distance carrier.

Some establishments may block direct dialing services, requiring guests to pay the price. To counteract this policy, AT&T's Teleplan Plus is negotiating with hotel chains to eliminate barriers to their USADirect and conventional calling card calls. Another service, Executive TeleCard, enables callers to bypass hotel switchboards within or between 27 countries. A push-button phone is required for computerized access to a global "switch," with calls billed to major credit cards.

Until such services are available globally, calling alternatives that always work include a telephone credit card, calling collect, and using public telephones in hotel lobbies or local post offices. Alternatively, provide a copy of your itinerary to friends, family, or business colleagues so they can call you, or originate the call yourself requesting they call you back right away.

DON'T FORGET TO SEND A POSTCARD

Sending or receiving correspondence while overseas seems a fairly straightforward affair, but keep in mind certain key points:

- Concierge desks will sometimes send your postcards and letters by regular mail, not air mail as you requested, keeping the difference in postage cost for themselves. If possible, buy stamps and send correspondence from local post offices.
- If you are traveling for an extended period, you may want to arrange to pick up mail or messages at key points on your itinerary. General Delivery (Poste Restante) services at post offices in most countries will hold mail for you. Contact your destination's tourist information office before your departure for procedural details.
- Some banks and international credit card companies will send and receive mail for customers from any one of their local offices overseas. Contact your bank or credit card issuer for a list of such offices.
- U.S. embassies and consulates overseas typically will not accept mail for citizens; exceptions include emergencies. Carry a

list of embassy and consulate addresses for cities you'll be visiting just in case.

MAKING SURE YOU'RE PLUGGED IN

Electrical standards differ from the U.S. where 110-volt, 60-cycle AC (alternating current) is the norm. Far too many hair dryers and electric razors have burned out from higher voltage outlets, which *are never marked* as such.

Some hotels and other accommodations have installed outlets that allow guests to switch back and forth. And some appliances provide dual voltage settings for this very purpose. Since these situations are still rare, the safest bet is to purchase a set of electrical converters, which are inexpensive and lightweight. For additional information about electricity converters, see Appendix C.

For travelers staying in less conventional lodgings, be sure to bring along an extension cord, which can provide the distance needed from the wall outlet to the sink and mirror.

A FEW FINAL THOUGHTS ABOUT LODGING

- If you're venturing out on your own, without benefit of travel planning, consider booking at least one night at a conventional hotel before you leave. Then, ask local residents for recommendations that suit your taste once you arrive (and have had a good night's sleep in a bed that's paid for).
- In Europe, some hotels and inns (especially the historic ones) don't provide bathrooms with toilets, requiring guests to skip down the hall. If you want a toilet in your room, specifically request one. Most European hotels below the "deluxe" class don't provide soap, and rarely furnish washcloths. And don't forget an extra roll of toilet tissue, just in case your lodgings run scarce of this necessity.
- Bring your own film. Film purchased in hotel lobbies or local shops can produce blurred photos. Also, special films—high speed or black and white—can be hard to find, especially during peak seasons, so bring along some extra rolls.
- Tourist information offices of the country you plan on visiting will usually provide free brochures and pamphlets. Some might also rate hotels, inns, and lodgings according to the facilities available at that property. See the listing of these offices in Appendix B.

CHAPTER **5**

MONEY MATTERS MATTER

Grace was finally on her way to Paris—a vacation she had dreamed about for years and carefully planned for six months. But as she dashed for the international terminal at Chicago's O'Hare Airport, it struck her: "Foreign currency . . . I didn't get any foreign currency." A quick scan of the terminal revealed a currency exchange window, three-deep with travelers having the same idea. To avoid any further delay, she decided it would be simple just to exchange traveler's checks once she landed at Orly Airport in Paris. Upon deplaning, Grace was greeted by a sign in the exchange's window that read "Banks on Strike."

Near panic, Grace decided she could buy a light breakfast at an airport coffee shop, pay with a $50 traveler's check and receive the change back in French francs—at least enough to get her into the city where her crisis could be resolved. After some amount of convincing, Grace successfully persuaded the coffee shop manager to let her make the exchange.

In the end, Grace made it to her hotel, only to be told that the Parisian bank with the best exchange rate was miles away, requiring delay and disruption to the itinerary she'd planned so carefully.

A major difference between traveling domestically and traveling abroad requires that we *think about* how we'll pay for each phase of our trip. Although many U.S. destinations may *seem* like exotic foreign destinations, business is still transacted in dollars and cents. As a result, *preparing* to travel abroad must involve considering our monetary needs, both cash and credit, because being caught off-guard can be both expensive and inconvenient, as Grace discovered once she arrived in Paris.

Begin by sitting down with a sharp pencil and reviewing your monetary needs in the context of your itinerary. (*Hint:* You should have your itinerary fairly well set at this point.) The key here is matching your activities and their related expenses with a suitable form of payment—credit or charge card, traveler's checks, foreign currency, and so on.

For instance, a bed-and-breakfast lodging in the mountains of Switzerland probably won't accept a credit or charge card as payment. Conversely, every major hotel in Japan will. Check with your travel agent or tourist information office for accepted practices within your destination.

If possible, using all appropriate monetary instruments in combination is the most effective *way to pay:* credit cards for such items as airline tickets, package tours, lodgings, car rentals, and meals; traveler's checks for day-to-day expenses and to pay proprietors who won't accept credit cards; foreign currency for day-to-day purchases, such as a newspaper, subway tokens, souvenirs, museum fees, and bellmen's tips; and some U.S. dollars for emergency purposes.

PLANNING YOUR MONETARY NEEDS

When determining your travel costs and how you'll pay for them, start with the big-ticket items on your itinerary: airline tickets, accommodations, food, and local transportation. But don't forget extra expenses that are inevitably encountered when traveling, such as sightseeing costs, souvenirs and other shopping expenses, recreational activities (golf, tennis, skiing), cultural activities (museums, theater, opera) and tips, among others.

Attempt to work with your travel agent or a tourist information office to roughly estimate expenses before you leave. That way you'll be prepared with enough cash and credit power to cover *all* your costs. And keep in mind that costs will vary, based on fluctuations in the foreign exchange rate for each country you visit. Depending upon your destination, the cost of something in dollars today may be quite different by the time you embark on your journey.

Dealing in international currencies is often mind-boggling, but international banks can help.

CREDIT AND CHARGE CARDS

Using "plastic" to pay is a convenience of our modern age, one that we've become accustomed to for many large and small purchases. With *credit* cards, consumers are extended a revolving line of credit that can be paid off on time, while *charge* cards require all balances be paid in full at month's end. When traveling abroad, your credit and charge cards also can be used to obtain cash advances, secure reservations, and verify identity as well.

In fact, experts are now advising travelers to use credit cards to satisfy their foreign currency needs. The reason: Credit cards offer wholesale foreign exchange rates when converting currencies, while establishments that exchange U.S. dollars and traveler's checks into foreign currency can levy hefty surcharges to do so. (See "Accessing Your Cash" for more information.)

While using a credit card to pay for purchases and exchange money abroad is convenient, there's one clear risk involved. Credit card companies reserve the right to decide *when* they'll make the currency conversion calculations, from foreign currency to dollars. As a result, you may be charged more or less than you anticipated for a purchase made overseas.

TRAVEL TIP   Some credit card companies add "conversion fees" to each transaction converted from foreign currency to U.S. dollars. Check with your card issuers before you leave home to determine if you'll be subject to such charges so you're not surprised when the bill comes. ■

Another credit card practice that can prove problematic while traveling involves hotels that "block" an amount against your card at check-in. Because they're afraid you'll exceed your spending limits while visiting their destination, they can block up to $2,000 in charges. One way around this practice is to take a second credit card along, allowing that one to be imprinted at check-in and switching all *real* charges to the original card at check-out. (Leave all unnecessary credit cards at home. And record the numbers of the credit cards that you do bring and keep the list in a separate place from the cards.)

Just as important in using charge and credit cards abroad is keeping track of your purchases so you don't exceed your limit. Travelers, in rare cases, have been arrested overseas for mistakenly exceeding their credit limit. Avoid any problems by calculating your credit card needs, checking your balance, and contacting your card issuer for a short-term (or long-term) credit line extension to cover your purchases, if necessary. Splitting charges between two cards may be another alternative.

TRAVEL TIP For travelers who regularly use credit cards to make purchases at home, consider signing up with American Express or Citicorp Diner's Club, the two best charge cards for earning travel credits while still on the ground. Also, many credit cards now offer frequent flyer mileage points when used to make purchases. And all such cards offer other perks, such as insurance, ATM access, and hotel discounts. ■

TRAVELER'S CHECKS

To avoid carrying large amounts of cash, most travelers continue to make noncredit purchases overseas with traveler's checks, which celebrated their 100th anniversary in 1991. Long touted as the safest way to carry cash while you travel, traveler's checks have been issued predominantly in U.S. dollars and offered by five major companies—Citicorp, American Express, Visa, Master-Card/Thomas Cook, and Bank of America/Barclays Bank.

However, one practice that's gaining in availability and popularity is foreign currency-denominated traveler's checks. While they can be more complicated and inconvenient to purchase—requiring foreign exchange up front and not always available at all banks—foreign currency travelers checks offer myriad benefits.

First, they're acceptable *anywhere* in the countries you may be visiting, despite what Karl Malden says on television about U.S. dollar traveler's checks. Second, they're more convenient once overseas because they eliminate the need to make currency conversions during your trip.

Foreign currency traveler's checks are available in an ever-widening array of currencies, including Australian dollars, Canadian dollars, Dutch guilders, British pounds, French francs, German marks, Hong Kong dollars, Japanese yen, Swiss francs, and Spanish pesetas. Usually, you can purchase them at the same place you buy foreign currency, and some services offer them in the same package.

TRAVEL TIP Cashing U.S. dollar traveler's checks can be an expensive proposition. Whenever possible, cash traveler's checks at a bank, travel service office like American Express or Thomas Cook, or a reliable currency exchange office, where exchange rates and service charges are more favorable than restaurants, hotels or shops. Avoid shopping with U.S. dollar traveler's checks; convert them into local currency first. ■

Traveler's checks also aren't a good way to pay for meals or hotel charges—unless they're denominated in the currency of the country you're visiting. Some restaurants and merchants levy 5 percent to 10 percent surcharges for accepting U.S. dollar traveler's checks, while hotels sometimes take an extra 3 percent to 5 percent, and car rental agencies and airlines up to 8 percent.

TRAVEL TIP When purchasing traveler's checks in foreign currency denominations, keep in mind that it's better to exchange currency only once. To convert it back, you'll incur more fees and you'll probably lose money. If you're in doubt, you may prefer to carry a combination of foreign currency *and* U.S. dollar traveler's checks, so you're prepared either way. ■

TRAVELER'S CHECK SAFETY

The first thing to remember when purchasing traveler's checks is to sign on the first signature line. Do this before you leave the bank because they're typically not refundable if they are lost or stolen while they are unsigned. Never countersign until you're ready to make a purchase.

A traveler's check purchase agreement—which includes the serial number, denomination, the date and location of the issuing bank or agency, and instructions in case of loss or theft—should always be kept separate from the checks themselves. Consider making several photocopies of the agreement and stashing them in several places in your luggage. That way, if a mishap occurs, you can get replacements quickly and easily.

Obtaining replacement checks depends on your location, the time of day, and other particulars. Usually, it's nothing more than calling the check issuer's toll-free refund number (some provide local numbers, but sometimes a call back to the United States is required). Replacement checks or a refund will be issued by a local bank, sales office, or even a Western Union office or hotel designated as a refund center. The key to preparing in this case is to always have that toll-free number at your disposal. Write it down somewhere that you'll remember, and keep it with other important travel documents. The number can also be accessed in case you're having trouble cashing your traveler's checks.

FOREIGN CURRENCY

When it comes to carrying cash overseas, several options exist. Purchasing some amount of foreign currency before you leave home is highly advisable, especially for those first few hours on the ground and perhaps the first weekend, but also for incidental purchases, local transportation and tipping. The amount of currency you carry with you depends on when and where you arrive (weekends and early mornings may find airport exchange windows closed), where you're going, how long you're staying, and the availability of ATM machines.

The best exchange rates and most convenience are offered by the large, international banks, such as Citibank and others that may exist in your hometown or city. (In smaller towns, many local banks have correspondent relationships with larger banks for this and other similar reasons.) Such institutions offer foreign currency exchange services. Citibank, for instance, offers "World Wallet," a package of foreign currency and traveler's checks that also includes helpful travel and banking tips for numerous destinations. Up to $5,000 can be exchanged using World Wallet, and Citibank customers can order it by phone, requesting overnight delivery to the branch nearest their home or office. Other financial service and travel institutions, such as Reusch International and Thomas Cook, offer similar services.

Don't be confused by exchange rates published in newspapers. These are "interbank rates," and represent the *wholesale* exchange rate that banks and brokerage houses receive when exchanging large blocks of money. Consumers are offered a *retail* rate, which always includes a mark-up to cover administrative costs.

The single strongest arguments for exchanging dollars into foreign currency *before* you go are time savings and convenience. Why spend the first few hours—or any significant portion of your trip—hunting for the best exchange rate? And this assumes you'll know a *good* exchange rate when you see one. To make it easiest on yourself, get some drachma, francs, or pesos before you go.

TRAVEL TIP   Many currencies are considered undesirable to U.S. banks, mostly because of their obscurity or widely fluctuating nature. As a result, you may be able to get some denominations of such currencies before you go, but may not be able to convert them back into dollars when you return. Check with your bank about the "convertibility" of the currency you desire, and take their advice on whether to get some or not. ■

Since searching for good exchange rates can waste precious time, it's best to exchange currency before you go.

If you must purchase foreign currency abroad, don't stop at the first exchange office you see when you reach your destination—you'll probably get better rates by shopping around. The most expensive money changers include airport windows, hotel front desks, and some exchange houses. They usually offer poor exchange rates, and charge fees of up to 10 percent. Banks are often the least expensive, offering better rates, which are frequently posted in windows.

Just as in the United States, overseas banks are typically closed on weekends, national holidays, and in some countries, religious holidays. On normal business days, some banks—especially in Europe—are closed for several hours in the middle of the day, usually to coincide with the mid-day meal.

TRAVEL TIP   It's better to exchange larger amounts of currency infrequently, rather than smaller quantities constantly. This will reduce the amount of exchange fees and service charges you will incur when converting money. ■

In many countries, dollars are preferred to their local currency, so making purchases in dollars may be more advantageous. Also, as mentioned earlier, nonconvertible currencies will have no value once you return to the United States, so exchange just enough to cover your needs.

Above all, avoid private currency transactions. In some countries, you risk more than being swindled or stuck with counterfeit currency, you risk arrest. Avoid the black market. Learn and obey the local currency laws wherever you go, keeping in mind that some countries regulate the amount of local currency you can bring into or take out of the country. Others require that you exchange a minimum amount of currency. For currency regulations, check with a bank, foreign exchange firm, your travel agent, or the tourist information offices of the countries you wish to visit.

And, if you leave or enter the United States with more than $10,000 in monetary instruments of any kind, you must file a report—Customs Form 4790—with U.S. Customs at the time of your departure. Failure to comply can result in civil and criminal proceedings.

ACCESSING YOUR CASH: THE AGE OF ATM WITHDRAWALS

In most major cities in Europe and Asia, automated teller machines (ATMs) now accept some American ATM cards, charge cards, and credit cards for cash withdrawals. Like credit card transactions, these machines offer wholesale exchange rates (typically better than other establishments) to Americans who withdraw cash in foreign currency from their hometown bank accounts while overseas.

Despite favorable rates, cash dispensed through an ATM incurs a service charge. Each institution that issues the ATM card sets its own specific terms—normally a $1 to $2 charge per withdrawal regardless of the amount you withdraw—so checking with your bank is advisable. Most also limit how much money you can withdraw per day.

Travelers whose banks are connected to the Cirrus® or Plus® ATM network can easily access ATMs abroad. To see if you belong, check the back of your ATM card. If either logo appears, you should be able to use their ATMs abroad. Access to the Cirrus network is available through about 21,000 terminals abroad; Plus is accessible through 24,000. However, overseas ATMs will only accept a four-digit Personal Identification Number (PIN). If your current PIN is more than four numbers or is made up of letters, you must apply for a new one.

Finding an ATM that accepts your card overseas can be a problem. No universal lists exist, so contact your bank for a directory of foreign banks where your particular ATM card is accepted.

Many credit and charge cards, such as MasterCard (called Eurocard in Western Europe), Visa, Diner's Club, or American Express, also offer cash advances to cardholders through ATMs in many countries abroad. (Visa and the Plus ATM network are working to make their two systems compatible, while MasterCard and Cirrus are doing the same.)

If you carry the American Express card and want to use it for cash withdrawals overseas, you must apply for a special PIN in advance to use one of their 20,000 cash-dispensing machines outside the United States. American Express charges a service fee that is equivalent to 2 percent of the transaction, imposing a minimum service fee of $2.50 up to a maximum of $10. By contrast, Diners Club typically charges a transaction fee of 4 percent. If your local bank's ATM card is not connected to either the Cirrus or Plus network, using American Express for this purpose may be best for you, especially since any problems that arise can be easily resolved at one of American Express' many offices around the world. For more information on the American Express service, call (800)227-4669.

TRAVEL TIP When using credit cards to access cash, understand that such transactions are considered loans and begin accruing interest immediately at a typical average rate of 18.5 percent. However, if you pay your credit card bill in full every month, this interest charge can be minimal. And, cash advances continue accruing interest until your entire card balance is paid off. ■

Finally, one major difference between credit/charge cards and ATM cards: if you lose your cards while abroad, credit and charge cards generally can be replaced easily; ATM cards are difficult to replace while you're away from home. So, keep your wits about you when carrying and using them.

EMERGENCY FUNDS

In case of emergency, pack a few personal checks which can oftentimes be cashed at a local American Express office or U.S. embassy or consulate. Also, take along the telephone number of your local bank in the event you need to have money wired, which will take several *business* days at a minimum.

The U.S. State Department can help, too. Its Office of Overseas Citizens Services will accept money and send it by wire transfer or overnight delivery to a trust account in the traveler's name at the nearest U.S. embassy or consulate. For a free information sheet about the service, *Sending Money to Overseas Citizens Services,* call the State Department at (202)647-5225, or fax your request to (202)647-3000.

THE VALUE-ADDED TAX (VAT)

In planning your monetary needs for a European trip, you'll need to consider the value-added tax (VAT), which is added to all purchases at rates varying from 3 percent to 30 percent. VAT paid for hotel rooms and meals is not reimbursable, but VAT imposed on retail purchases can be reimbursed to visitors—provided you meet a minimum amount to qualify for a rebate and you're willing to endure complicated refund processes.

Not every retail establishment permits VAT rebates; those that do typically display signage saying so. The VAT refund is only for items you can present at your port of departure's customs counter, along with receipts and VAT refund forms. Refunds are made by mail if purchases were made with cash, or by crediting your charge/credit card.

Because VAT rates, rules and refunds vary from country to country, check with your destination's tourist information office before you leave to anticipate local circumstances. When formulating your itinerary, leave enough time to present your receipts to the airport or seaport VAT refund counter when you depart your destination. And be sure to pack merchandise that qualifies for the refund in a separate tote bag, so if you're asked to present the items, you can do so without tearing apart your luggage.

PREPARING FOR THE CUSTOMS PROCESS

Your ability to breeze through customs—when entering a new destination country or returning home—depends on the discretion of the customs officials you encounter and, quite frankly, the innocence of your face.

To lessen the chances of encountering customs headaches, be sure to:

• Register valuables you will take on your trip abroad with a U.S. airport Customs Office before you leave. Anything you will take that is manufactured abroad—cameras, jewelry, portable computers, and electronics—should be presented to the Customs office with proof of ownership (sales receipt, insurance policies, jewelry appraisals). Items that have serial numbers are especially important to document, since it will make your return with such items quicker and easier. The procedure can be time consuming, however, so be sure to allow at least one-half hour on the day of your departure, or—better yet—visit the airport Customs Office or a local Customs Office a few days before your trip.

• When packing for your trip, include a compact, empty bag that will fold easily into your large suitcase. Use it to pack all your purchases and gifts together. That way, should you be asked to present your purchases at Customs, you won't have to unpack everything in your suitcase.

• Keep all the receipts for your purchases together in an envelope or folder. In addition to the receipts, write a list of everything you buy on the folder or envelope front, including the items' U.S. dollar value and the amount you paid if purchased in a foreign currency. This list will come in handy when you're asked to complete a declaration form during your return flight or when asked questions as you pass through Customs.

• If you are returning with a gift and do not know its value, don't guess—ask a Customs official. Remember, these people are experts who know the true value of foreign-made goods.

You are allowed to bring $400 worth of merchandise into the U.S. duty free, provided you have been out of the country for at least 48 hours, you can present the purchases upon return, and you have not used the exemption within the past 30 days. The next $1,000 worth of items you bring back for personal use or as gifts are subject to duty at a flat rate of 10 percent (the amount of declarable goods varies if you visit parts of Central America, the Caribbean, and the U.S. insular possessions of American Samoa, Guam, and the U.S. Virgin Islands). There are numerous restrictions, however, as to the types and amounts of products you can bring into the United States.

Also remember that each and every country differs in customs regulations. Check with the tourist information offices of the countries you will visit *before you leave home* to determine if there are any restrictions you may encounter at your port of entry or departure.

The U.S. Customs Service offers these free brochures:

• *Know Before You Go—Customs Hints for Returning Residents;*
• *United States Customs Hints for Visitors;*

- *GSP and the Traveler* (products from certain developing countries under the Generalized System of Preferences which are granted duty preferences).

To request copies of these publications, write to U.S. Customs Service, Office of Public Information, P.O. Box 7407, Washington, DC 20044.

Other free publications to consult before your trip include:

- *Travelers Tips on Bringing Food, Plant, and Animal Product into the United States* from the U.S. Department of Agriculture, 613 Federal Bldg., 6505 Belcrest Road, Hyattsville, MD 20782;
- *Buyer Beware!* which provides general guidelines governing restrictions on imports of wildlife and wildlife products into the U.S., available from the Publications Unit, U.S. Fish and Wildlife Service, Office of Management Authority, 4401 N. Fairfax Dr., Room 420-C, Arlington, VA 22203;
- Additional information on importing wildlife and wildlife products can be obtained through TRAFFIC USA, World Wildlife Fund, 1250 24th Street, N.W., Washington, DC 20037; and
- If you will be living or working abroad for an extended period, contact your local IRS office for information on how to order publication 54, *Tax Guide for U.S. Citizens & Resident Aliens Abroad,* and publication 593, *Tax Highlights for U.S. Citizens and Residents Going Abroad.*

STAYING HEALTHY

Ann D. arrived in London on a Friday for her first trip abroad. Two days later, while crossing the street, she was struck by a bicyclist and fractured her pelvis. The next day, she canceled the rest of her vacation and made the painful journey home.

Carol C.'s story occurred on a tour of Switzerland. It began with stomach cramps, which grew steadily worse. A Swiss doctor diagnosed her ailment as appendicitis and suggested an immediate operation. Instead, Carol phoned her physician back in the United States who, after hearing about the lab results, advised that it could not possibly be appendicitis. Knowing Carol's medical history, he believed it was an attack of diverticulitis, which proved to be true. Carol cut her vacation short and returned to the United States.

Stories such as these turn dream vacations into painful nightmares. While neither could have been avoided, they represent common fears for many travelers.

BEFORE YOU GO

As with so much involving travel, to guarantee a successful trip, some of the most crucial steps are those you take before you ever set foot on a plane, train or ship. As you prepare for your trip, take these simple steps:

- See your doctor, especially if you suffer from any health problems, or will be visiting remote areas (see p. 68 for information about immunizations), or will be away for an extended period of time.
- Pack over-the-counter remedies—or prescriptions—that work best for you for headaches, backaches, and muscle soreness; upset stomach or motion sickness; diarrhea and constipation; sunburn; head colds or allergies.
- Pack a first aid kit, including band-aids, tweezer or a needle (for splinters), a thermometer, antiseptic, a small knife and scissors, and a first aid manual.
- Write out a traveler's medical record reflecting your current health conditions and other relevant information, and pack it in your suitcase in case of emergency. This record should include: your name, address, and date of birth; blood type

Over-the-counter medications can do the trick, but always check with your personal physician before traveling abroad.

(including Rh factor); recent immunizations with dates received; any medical conditions or allergies; any medications you are currently taking; your doctor's name, address, and telephone number; the name, address, and phone number of your insurance company; and, most importantly, the name, address and phone number of the person to contact in case of emergency (along with their relationship to you).

- Have a dental check-up before you leave.
- If you wear glasses, bring along a spare pair and a copy of your prescription (in the event your glasses are broken or lost), and carry it in your wallet or purse. If you wear contact lenses, bring along ample supplies—cleaning solution, soaking solution, and so on.
- If you wear a hearing aid, carry spare batteries.

If you suffer from diabetes, high blood pressure, cardiopulmonary disease, asthma, sinus trouble, or any illness, you should discuss your itinerary with your doctor before you go. If you have a special condition, you might consider talking to a specialist in travel medicine. For a referral in your community, contact the American Committee on Clinical Tropical Medicine and Traveler's Health, 148 Highland Avenue, Newton, MA 02165. If you send a 8 by 10 inch self-addressed envelope with 98¢ postage, they'll provide you with a directory of more than 100 travel-related doctors and clinics across the country.

For a complete listing of international medical information, order *Health Information for International Travel* from the U.S. Government Printing Office, Superintendent of Documents, P.O. Box 371954, Pittsburgh, PA 15250-7954, or check your local U.S. Government Printing Bookstore. The book includes vaccination certificate requirements, a table of immunization requirements, a geographical distribution of potential health hazards to travelers, and other health hints.

Other health information sources for travelers include the CDC's International Traveler's Hotline, (404)332-4559, and the Citizen's Emergency Center (for recordings of travel advisories), Bureau of Consular Affairs, Room 4811, N.S., U.S. Department of State, Washington, DC 20520, (202)647-5225.

There are also specific resources for allergy sufferers. They include the American Academy of Allergy and Immunology, 611 E. Wells Street, Milwaukee, WI 53202, (800)822-2762, which can supply names of allergists worldwide; and the Allergy and Asthma Network/Mothers of Asthmatics, 3554 Chain Bridge Road, Suite 200, Fairfax, VA 22030, (800)878-4403, which serves as a clearinghouse for information about allergies in the United States and abroad.

A SHOT IN THE ARM

One of the most common questions asked by international travelers is, "Which shots do I need?" But before we review travel-related immunizations, a quick note about ordinary immunizations, the ones most people receive as infants. Check your pediatric medical records first; then, ask your doctor about which shots you should make sure you've had to avoid common diseases. The following list details these illnesses and the approximate time you should allow before departure:

Disease	Time Required
Measles/Mumps/Rubella	2 weeks
Influenza	2 weeks
Pneumonia	2 weeks
Tetanus/diphtheria	4–6 weeks

If you plan to travel to Canada, Europe, Australia, or New Zealand, you'll usually find little risk of disease. But the danger of disease varies widely in parts of Africa, Asia, Central and South America, Mexico, the Caribbean, the Middle East and the South Pacific—and many nations in those places require written proof of vaccinations for *yellow fever* and *cholera*. Your doctor should be able to tell you where to go for these important vaccinations.

For the most up-to-date information on vaccines (and other health concerns) when traveling abroad, contact the Centers for Disease Control (CDC), U.S. Department of Health and Human Services, 1600 Clifton Road, N.E., Atlanta, GA 30333, (404)639-3311. The CDC provides the latest worldwide health information on diseases/epidemics, immunizations and precautionary measures for travelers.

In some countries, mosquitoes and other insects carry yellow fever and cholera, so check before you go about necessary immunizations.

TRAVEL TIP Women who are pregnant should know there is no documentation of safety for most vaccines (tetanus being a notable exception). Therefore, if you are pregnant, you should not be immunized without first consulting your doctor. ■

Another source for information about vaccination requirements is Immunization Alert (IA), which can provide personalized computer printouts of required immunizations based on your itinerary, or IBM (DOS and Windows) or Macintosh versions of IA's complete database on computer disk. IA also offers a publication entitled *General Comments on Disease Prevention While Traveling,* and a 210-page guidebook entitled *Foreign Travel & Immunization Guide* authored by IA's founder, Dr. Kenneth Dardick. For additional information, contact Immunization Alert at 93 Timber Drive, Storrs, CT 06268, (800)584-1999 or (203)487-0611.

YOUR PERSONAL PRESCRIPTIONS

Because of the severe penalties in many foreign countries for possessing illegal drugs, and because you don't want to be caught without proper medication, let's expand a bit on this point.

If you're taking any medication at all on a trip, take these extra steps to avoid problems:

- Ask your doctor for a statement and prescription form if you are using injectable medication, such as insulin. Some countries prohibit the use or importation of syringes, needles, or narcotic medications, and having documentation from your physician may be required at the port of entry.
- Also ask your doctor for a letter describing your specific health condition(s) and applicable prescriptions in the event you should have to replace any medication while traveling.
- Carry medication in its original prescription bottle, with the labels properly affixed. And take more medication than you need—for various reasons, some trips are extended.
- Take extra prescription forms listing generic and brand names, in case your medication is lost or taken from you. If you need help filling a prescription, call the U.S. embassy or consulate to recommend an English-speaking pharmacy.
- Carry your medication either on your person or in a carry-on bag; if your medication is packed in your luggage and the luggage is lost or misplaced, you may have a potentially dangerous problem.
- Get a desiccator—a tablet or capsule that's used to keep moisture away from medications that may decompose if damp. They're free at most U.S. pharmacies.
- Stick to brands you know when buying over-the-counter medicines, or ask the pharmacist for a suitable substitute. Above all, avoid local remedies.

These precautions make Customs processing easier. A doctor's certificate, however, may not suffice as authorization to transport *all* prescription drugs to *all* foreign countries. Travelers have innocently been arrested for drug violations when carrying items not considered to be narcotics into the United States. To ensure that you do not violate the drug laws of the countries you visit, consult the embassy or consulate of those countries for precise information before leaving the United States.

AVOIDING ILLNESS AND INJURY WHEN YOU TRAVEL

There are several things you can do to prevent both illness or injury and stay healthy when you travel.

When planning your itinerary, be sure you allow yourself enough time to get plenty of rest. Fatigue lowers the body's resistance and opens the doors to illness. And be sure your destinations won't adversely affect your health—especially pre-existing conditions that may already be personal health concerns. For instance, destinations with elevations of 10,000 feet or higher may cause problems for people with pulmonary or cardiac ailments. Visits to cities with high temperatures or humidity should be minimized or avoided if you are prone to dehydration.

After you've packed your travel health kit and found out about any special vaccinations or considerations, you may want to think about your transportation circumstances—especially if you're flying.

Being packed into an airplane, which recirculates the air breathed by several hundred people, is not a squeaky clean environment. Since smoking is still allowed on some international airlines, ask for a seat in the nonsmoking section, especially if you've got allergies or sensitive lungs.

If you suffer from back ailments, place a pillow or two behind the small of your back or neck, and recline your seat. Both can ensure your back doesn't end up in knots. In fact, several manufacturers make back and neck pillows small enough to carry, among them Body Care, P.O. Box 219, Ball Ground, GA 30107, (800)858-9888; Backsaver Products, 53 Jeffrey Ave., Holliston, MA 01746, (800)251-2225; and Magellan's Essentials for the Traveler, P.O. Box 5485, Santa Barbara, CA 93150-5485, (800)962-4943.

Take pressure off the spine by moving around during the flight (every two hours) and strolling the aisles. Also, use a small suitcase as a footrest to relieve spinal and hamstring stress.

Bring a sweater, or something warm, to ward off the inevitable drafts around your seat. And drink plenty of fluids—water preferably—to ward off dehydration. Keep in mind that alcohol can speed dehydration. Check with your doctor or pharmacist before your trip about bringing along motion or sea sickness remedies.

Suitcases with rollers—several small ones rather than one large one—can also prove less stressful on hikes through airports, train stations, and ports of call. And be careful how you snatch your luggage from the conveyer belts in baggage claim areas. The adventure you're looking for probably doesn't include traction.

PREVENTION IS THE BEST TACTIC

One of the most inconvenient, embarrassing, and debilitating travel-related problems is diarrhea. The best way to guard against it is by watching carefully what you eat or drink. Especially in warm-weather countries, stay away from these foods:

- Raw or inadequately cooked shellfish or seafood (for it to be safe, it must be boiled for eight minutes);
- Raw salads and fruit that haven't been thoroughly washed in clean water;
- Fruit that you can't peel yourself;
- Food that requires a lot of handling;
- Food that's been stored and reheated;
- Food left out in warm temperatures (like buffets); and
- Cold meats.

Everyone says, "Don't drink the water." And for good reason. Water, water, everywhere, and, while estimates vary, some experts say that almost 99 percent of the world's water is unsafe to drink. Here are some tips to follow when drinking water:

- Drink only water you know is safe, and boil water that's questionable in a small hotpot that can be easily stowed in your luggage.
- Never drink from public faucets, fountains, or the tap—nor use water from these sources to brush your teeth.
- Drink bottled water or canned drinks (and stick to known brands). Travelers with high blood pressure, heart, or kidney problems should check the mineral content of bottled water before drinking it.
- Drink only carbonated water that has a label and is sealed to prove that its contents have been bottled at a plant (locals in some countries put tap water in brand-name bottles). In some languages, "carbonated" translates to "gas."
- Don't drink directly out of bottles, soda, or beer cans, since their containers could be contaminated.
- Avoid drinks with ice cubes — even if the water is safe, ice may be made with contaminated water.

• Never drink from ponds, lakes, rivers, or streams. Be even more cautious in rural areas, where local water sources might not be purified as well as in big cities.

You *can* drink water if you purify it first by boiling, or with iodine. Add five drops of 2 percent tincture of iodine (which you can get from any pharmacy) per quart, or one drop per cup, and wait 20 minutes before drinking.

Along with taking precautions with food, it's also important to wash your hands frequently. Every time you pass or are near a wash basin, stop and wash your hands. Most germs are transported from hands to mouth, and when you're traveling, you often shake hands and touch public objects, like railings, handles, and doorknobs.

IF YOU DO GET SICK ABROAD

In most parts of Canada, Australia, Japan, or Western Europe, with abundant doctors, sophisticated facilities, and many people who speak English, you probably should be able to find the care you need.

As part of your health preparations, check with your insurance company regarding hospitalization and major medical coverage while abroad. Some do not apply outside the United States, and Medicare never makes payments to overseas health care providers.

While medical insurance for travelers is available (see Chapter 11 on Insurance), a number of organizations exist to help travelers with chronic ailments or illnesses requiring them to return home.

• The International Association for Medical Assistance to Travelers (IAMAT), 417 Center Street, Lewiston, NY 14092, (716)754-4883. IAMAT offers members an identification card that guarantees services from IAMAT-affiliated providers at fixed rates, a worldwide directory of English-speaking physicians, a traveler's clinical record form, a world immunization chart and world climate charts, including seasonal clothing recommendations. Be sure to contact IAMAT before your departure, however, to obtain your membership card should you need a referral for health care abroad.

• International Health Care Service, New York Hospital-Cornell Medical Center, 440 E. 69th Street, New York, NY 10021,

(212)746-1601. For a nominal fee with self-addressed envelope, this service provides the *International Health Care Travelers Guide,* which includes facts and advice on health care and diseases throughout the world.

• International SOS Assistance, P.O. Box 11568, Philadelphia, PA 19116, (800)523-8930, provides 24-hour emergency assistance, including telephone consultation for medical emergencies, referral to medical centers throughout the world, and emergency assistance for transportation of ill travelers or family members.

• Medic Alert Foundation, P.O. Box 1009, Turlock, CA 95381, (800)ID-ALERT, provides individuals with identification emblems that state health conditions that may not be easily observable. Once you are registered with Medic Alert, health care providers can call an emergency line 24 hours a day for detailed information about your personal medical history.

COMBATING JET LAG

Few travelers escape jet lag—those hangover-like blahs that hit after an overnight flight through two or three time zones. Here are some points to keep in mind that can diminish the effects of jet lag:

• Make a very long trip in several stages, when possible;
• Drink plenty of water and non-alcoholic beverages while en route by plane; and
• Eat lightly, avoid smoking, and stretch your legs as often as possible.

Dr. Charles Ehret, author of *Overcoming Jet Lag,* suggests an alternative, a special diet that he says combats the symptoms. Ehret's diet alternates proteins, carbohydrates, and caffeine for several days before the trip. He says the diet, combined with exercise, helps reset the body's biological clock.

Dr. Stephen Forsyth has another unique approach to resetting the body's clock. He suggests:

• The evening before the trip, eat a meal high in carbohydrates, such as pasta.
• The day of the flight and during the flight, eat nothing—no food, coffee/tea, nonprescription drugs, or alcohol. Drink lots of water and juice, then go to sleep.
• Before you land, freshen up and eat the breakfast snack.

- Once on the ground, eat a normal breakfast, get into the sun and avoid napping. This will restart your biological clock to its new time.

Forsyth says his formula isn't medically valid, but it's worked for him and hundreds of friends, colleagues, and clients. You can get a free pamphlet, *Defeating Jet Lag,* by writing P.O. Box 2975, Shawnee Mission, KS 66201-1375. Enclose a self-addressed, stamped envelope.

Additional resources for researching health concerns when traveling abroad include:

- *Health Guide for International Travelers* by Dr. Thomas Sakmar, Dr. Pierce Gardner and Dr. Gene Peterson, Passport Books, 1989, $5.95.
- *Staying Healthy in Asia, Africa, and Latin America* by Dirk Schroeder, Moon Publications, Chico, CA, 1993, $7.95.
- *The New Traveler's Health Guide* by Dr. Patrick J. Doyle, Dr. James E. Banta, Acropolis Books Ltd., $4.95.
- *Travel Safety* by Jack Adler and Thomas Tompkins, Hippocrene Books, 1988, $14.95.
- *Traveler's Health: How to Stay Healthy Abroad* by Dr. Richard Dawood, Viking Press, $18.00.
- *Health Information for International Travel,* Center for Disease Control, Superintendent of Documents, U.S. Government Printing Office, 1992, $6.50.

TRAVELING SAFELY

Marvin and Betty R. traveled to Amsterdam as part of their first trip outside the United States. While they were boarding a tour bus outside their hotel, a gentleman behind Marvin tapped him on the shoulder saying, "Do you know you have mustard all over the back of your jacket?" Marvin quickly removed his jacket and, with the help of the other man, found some tissues and did their best to repair the mess. Marvin thanked the man, put his jacket back on and boarded the bus. Two hours later, at the first stop, when Marvin reached for his wallet, he discovered it was missing. His passport was also gone. He had kept both in an inside pocket of his jacket. After a thorough search, the driver suggested they report the loss to local police. There, a Dutch police officer merely shook his head and said, "Oh, the old mustard trick again." It was then Marvin and Betty learned that a common trick of local thieves was to purposely smear mustard on the back of a traveler's jacket, "help" him clean the mess, and, in the process, steal valuables from the pockets.

Unfortunately, the "mustard trick" is just one of a hundred ways a long-awaited trip abroad can be ruined. Theft, accidents, civil unrest, even terrorism and hijackings can also occur.

SAFETY TIPS BEFORE YOU LEAVE HOME

TIP #1: Pay attention to government warnings. The U.S. State Department issues "travel advisories" on specific countries where dangers are high. For example, at the start of the Persian Gulf War in January 1991, a strong "travel warning" was issued for Americans traveling any place in the world. Then in June 1993, after U.S. airplanes bombed Iraq, it issued a "worldwide advisory" to "exercise greater than usual caution" when traveling abroad. This type of advisory is considered a "reminder to people that acts against Americans could occur and when there are good reasons to believe there could be heightened tensions." At other times, the U.S. State Department warns about traveling into specific countries, such as Afghanistan and Nicaragua when civil wars were being waged in those countries.

TRAVEL TIP To learn about these travel warnings, whether they deal with natural disasters, disease outbreaks, acts of terrorism, international conflict, or civil unrest in specific countries, contact: Citizens Emergency Center, Overseas Citizens Services, U.S. Department of State, 2201 C St., N.W., Room 4800, Washington, D.C. 20520, (202)647-5225. Travel advisories are given on a recording 24 hours a day. ■

TIP #2:   Write away for copies of these four excellent publications issued by the U.S. State Department:

• A brochure titled *A Safe Trip Abroad*. This offers tips on guarding valuables, personal and vehicle security, and protecting against terrorism in a hijacking situations. It also provides information on the extent of assistance provided abroad by U.S. embassies and consulates. The cost is $1.

• Also, obtain a copy of the U.S. State Department's *Key Officers of Foreign Service Posts*. This provides contact names and addresses for all U.S. embassies, missions, and consulates abroad. This listing, which can be especially useful for business travelers, is updated three times annually. For copies contact the U.S. Government Printing Office, P.O. Box 371954, Pittsburgh, PA 15250, (202)783-3238.

• Two helpful pamphlets are *Crisis Abroad—What the State Department Does* and *U.S. Consuls Help Americans Abroad*. They can be obtained by sending a self-addressed stamped envelope to the U.S. Department of State, CA/P, Room 5807, Washington, D.C. 20520-4818.

TIP #3:   Ask your travel agent for additional information about safety measures for the specific country or countries you plan to visit. Check your local library for the most recent magazine and newspaper articles on the country you plan to visit, especially news items pertaining to safety.

TIP #4:   Copy, copy, copy. This means make copies of every document you consider valuable. This means your airline ticket, itinerary, credit cards, passport, traveler's check purchase agreement, driver's license, and other such personal documents. In fact, make two sets of copies—one to leave with friends or relatives at home, and one to stash in your luggage to take with you. These copies become invaluable if any of the originals are lost or stolen.

TIP #5:   Leave a list of the following information with a friend, co-worker, or relative: Name of your personal physician, name of your attorney, location of your will, and name of your insurance agents. This way you can travel comfortably knowing you are prepared for any emergency.

TIP #6: Leave valuable pieces of personal jewelry at home. An expensive watch or dazzling pieces of jewelry become a beacon to potential thieves. If you must take expensive jewelry along, make certain you have adequate insurance coverage and then plan to discipline yourself to place it in hotel safe deposit boxes or room or cabin safes, as soon as you arrive, and wear them with discretion.

TIP #7: Because business travelers are attractive targets for theft and even kidnapping, remove all company decals and other identification from your luggage if you are traveling on business; establish telephone "codes" with your home office and family; and leave full details of your itinerary and contact numbers with responsible people in your office.

SAFETY ON AIRPLANES

Question: *What is the single most important safety factor when aboard an aircraft of any kind?*

Answer: Buckling your seat belt. Ranking closely behind are paying attention to the safety instructions given by flight attendants before each flight, and noting where the nearest emergency exit is located. The flight attendants' instructions always explain how seat belts work (so there is no excuse for not using one), what happens in case of cabin decompression (oxygen masks drop down), and what to do if the plane is forced down over water (your seat cushion is a flotation device).

Question: *Where is the safest place to sit on an airplane?*

Answer: Nearest an emergency exit. These rows usually have more leg room as well. However, current regulations require that passengers seated in the emergency row be physically capable of removing the emergency hatch when instructed to do so. That means that the very elderly, handicapped, or the very young (15 or under) are directed away from this row. Incidentally, be careful about being seated in the row immediately in front of the emergency exit; the reason is that these seats do not recline (which in emergencies would partially obstruct exits); but a seat that does not recline means an uncomfortable seat for long trips.

Question: *What else can I do to improve my safety aboard an aircraft?*

Answer: According to travel writer Linda Pulliam, 60 percent of the deaths in crashes are caused by broken seats or flying debris. While you can't do anything about broken seats, you can avoid placing heavy objects in the overhead compartments. During turbulence or in a crash, the hatches could come open and those heavy objects could whip around the cabin like popcorn in a corn popper.

Question: *What are the chances of lightning hitting the airplane?*

Answer: While no statistics are made public, according to *The Wall Street Journal,* "safety experts say that on average each commercial airliner is struck by lightning once a year." That means there are about 4,000 strikes a year. The president of a lightning technology firm claims when lightning strikes an airplane, "You definitely know it. The plane jolts the same way a car does when driving over a bump real fast." The jolt is followed by a brilliant white flash. However, severe damage to commercial airliners is rare. The reason is that aircraft are designed to channel the lightning along a harmless path and away from fuel lines. Also, key

Lightning can occasionally strike airplanes, but rarely does any damage.

wires and control boards have special shields around them to
avoid damage.

SAFETY DO'S AND DON'TS WHEN STAYING IN A HOTEL

Fire and theft are the two most worrisome hazards when staying
in hotels. Fortunately, while staying at a hotel, there are many
common-sense precautions you can take to improve your safety
in either eventuality.

Do:

- Take a few moments to study escape routes (both up and
  down) in case of fire as soon as you're settled in your room.
  Experienced travelers count the doors between their room and
  the nearest fire exit door on the basis that during a fire the
  hallway will be filled with smoke.
- Always use all of the locking devices on the door when you are
  in your room.
- Place the "Do Not Disturb" sign on the outside of your door
  whether you are in the room or not. Another trick is to leave
  the TV or radio on when you leave the room. The combination
  of the sign and the sound might be enough disincentive for a
  room thief.
- Place all valuables in the hotel safe deposit box.
- Check the markings on faucets. Test which is "hot" and which
  is "cold." The reason is that the letter "C" in many countries
  stands for "hot" (caldo, caliente, chaud, etc.) This also translates into a possible scalding if you turn the wrong handle and
  step into the tub.

Don't:

- Open your door to anyone until you look through the view-port
  (if there is one) to verify who it is. If there is no view-port or
  peep-hole, keep the safety chain on the door until you identify
  the caller.
- Announce that you need to rent a safe deposit box when checking in. Do that later, quietly.
- Smoke in bed. This is the most common cause of fires in hotels
  around the world.
- Use side entrances when returning to your hotel late in the
  evening. Always use the main entrance and be observant when
  walking through parking lots.
- Use the "Please Make Up This Room" sign unless absolutely necessary; it announces to thieves that the room is probably empty.

Hotel Fire Safety Tips to Memorize

- Many guidebooks suggest you book a room between the second and seventh floors because fire equipment in most countries cannot reach higher than those floors.
- If the hotel fire alarm rings, leave your room immediately. Don't hesitate, wondering if it's a false alarm. And be sure to take your room key with you.
- Don't use the elevators; you could get stranded.
- If you hear the fire alarm or smell smoke, feel the door of your room. If it's hot, don't open it.
- If the hallway is full of smoke, close your door, and put a wet towel across the bottom crack. If you must leave the room, place a wet towel over your mouth and crawl along the floor to avoid heavy smoke.

In hotels overseas, fire safety still lags behind U.S. standards. If you want to be extra cautious about fire protection and other safety precautions at your hotel and, if a travel agent is booking your hotel reservations, ask about the following:

- Does the hotel have a sprinkler system?
- Does it have smoke and heat detectors in each room?
- What other information is available on security provisions for guests? Examples: Closed-circuit TV security cameras; magnetically imprinted room keycards; 24-hour telephone switchboard.

Another consideration is to carry with you a small smoke detector and batteries along with other security devices.

PROTECTING YOURSELF AGAINST THEFT

The only thing faster than the speed of light is how quickly pickpockets can reach inside a jacket, unzip a pocket, dip a hand inside, and withdraw a wallet.

Here is just one ploy showing how these faster-than-the-eye-can-follow-encounters can occur: Children carrying newspapers crowd around, imploring an intended victim to buy one. They press against their target, distract him or her, and then move on to the next "customer." In those five seconds, those lightning-fast tykes can relieve their victim of enough money to equal a month's income in their country—maybe even a year's pay. (Incidentally, this is exactly what happened to writer Bill Bryson during a trip to Italy; he lost $1,500 in traveler's checks.)

Thieves around the world find other ingenious ways to rob and steal. In Bogota, Colombia, for instance, drivers of automobiles have learned to avoid signaling turns by extending their arms out the window. Reason: Street thieves grab their wrist watches. Drivers there resorted to locking car doors and keeping windows rolled almost to the top. Faced with that, some criminals responded by forcing live snakes through the window openings which—understandably—causes drivers to stop instantly and scramble out of the car. At that point, the thief merely enters the car and drives off.

These modern-day highwaymen exist in every country and city where tourists and business people visit. Further, their techniques are becoming more audacious and more violent. Drug users, for instance, are turning to bold physical attacks to feed their addictions. In Spain, it is reported they have even brandished blood-stained syringes and threatened to plunge the needles into their victims, thus playing on the fear of AIDS.

Authorities in every country issue the same advice: The only way to minimize and avoid such mishaps is to be cautious and use common sense.

Here is a list of just a few common sense suggestions:

- Begin your precautions in advance of your trip: Buy traveler's checks (see Chapter 5), and make copies of your airline tickets, passport, and credit cards as described in previous chapters.
- Buy concealable wallets and pouches. While "fanny" packs are better than free-swinging purses, the belts for these pouches can still be cut and whisked away. Lacking these devices, the simplest precaution is for women to carry purses tightly against their bodies, placing the straps across their chest. Men should carry wallets in trouser side pockets which are deeper and more difficult for a thief to reach into. Another trick is to wrap several rubber bands around a wallet; that makes it more difficult to slip the wallet out of a trouser pocket.

TRAVEL TIP There is now a wide variety of hideable pouches and carriers available at affordable prices. Visit a luggage store or travel specialty store in your area. A list of Rand McNally's retail locations appears in Appendix D; these stores are well stocked with these items. ∎

- Wherever possible, avoid creating the perception that you *are* a tourist or visiting business person. Minimize this perception by:
  - Removing those old, tattered name tags provided by tour groups and business conventions.
  - Not displaying expensive watches, jewelry, and cameras.
  - Avoiding poorly lighted streets late at night.
  - Avoiding solo explorations. Try to walk in small groups, and stay away from crowded situations where people will jostle or brush up against you. Pickpockets often operate in groups, especially in public places like museums, airports, terminals, and at festive rallies.
  - Being observant; being aware. Thieves look for victims who are engrossed in sightseeing or involved in discussions. Be wary whenever anyone touches you.
  - Being alert when distractions occur. Examples: someone asks you to take their photograph; a fight breaks out near you; someone stops you and asks directions. Often these are planned distractions to cover a pickpocket's activities.

Finally, this note of consolation: The authors have a combined total of 55 years of world travel under their belts. Neither has ever experienced a serious mishap such as an airplane accident, hotel fire, theft, or assault. We routinely practice many of the safeguards listed on these pages.

OTHER SAFETY DO'S & DON'TS

Here is some general advice for any country or any situation:

- Do avoid looking like an American. That means putting away those sweatshirts with university logos, baseball caps, and other obvious American labels.
- Do be polite and low-key. Avoid loud conversations and arguments in public. Bear in mind that you are a guest in foreign countries.
- Do exchange money only at authorized agent locations.

Above all, try to avoid looking like obvious American tourists.

Even though black market exchanges may be extremely attractive, avoid the temptation.

- Do travel in small groups of four to six when sightseeing. Thieves tend to prey on singles, couples, and larger groups.
- Don't deal in drugs. Penalties for mere possession of even small amounts of marijuana or cocaine are severe—in some countries it means immediate long-term imprisonment.
- Don't carry a package aboard an airplane for another person unless you know the person extremely well, and you know exactly what is contained inside.
- Don't use taxis that are unmetered or appear to be unregistered.
- Don't leave your baggage or cameras inside a rented automobile where they can be seen.

In conclusion, this true story might be titled "Lightning Does Strike Twice." Two married Argentine couples were visiting Rio de Janiero, Brazil, on vacation. While walking along the famous beachfront one evening after dinner, they suddenly found themselves surrounded by a gang of youths who demanded their money. After emptying pockets and purses, the gang disappeared. Scared and shaken, the foursome hurried back to their hotel, reported the thefts to authorities, and headed directly to their rooms—only to exit the elevator and discover another thief attempting to break into their room!

HELP FROM THE U.S. GOVERNMENT

For help or information involving foreign travel, these U.S. State Department numbers can be helpful:

- In emergency situations, contact the Citizens Emergency Center at (202)647-5225 between 8:15 A.M. and 10 P.M. weekdays. At other times, call the State Department Operations Center at (202)647-1512.
- For non-emergency questions, contact the Citizens Consular Services at (202)647-3444. Examples of non-emergency matters are child adoptions, marriages overseas, judicial assistance, and so on.

Following is a list of services provided by American Consuls stationed abroad:

- First, you should register at the Consular Section of the nearest U.S. embassy or consulate if you find yourself in a country experiencing civil unrest or undergoing a natural disaster; or, if you plan to go to a country where there are no U.S. officials, you should register in an adjacent country; and, finally, if you plan to stay in any country for longer than one month.

- If you become destitute while abroad, the U.S. consul can help you get in touch with your family, friends, bank, or employer and advise them how to send funds for you.
- If you should become ill while abroad, the U.S. consul can provide a list of local doctors, dentists, clinics, and hospitals.
- The U.S. consul will also offer information on marriages, births, adoptions, and deaths of a U.S. citizen.

TRAVEL TIP Consular officers cannot act as travel agents, information bureaus, banks or law enforcement officers. U.S. federal law forbids a consular officer from acting as your lawyer. Further, they cannot find you employment; get you visas, residence permits or driving permits; act as interpreters; search for missing luggage, call your credit card company or bank, or replace stolen traveler's checks. ■

RECOMMENDED READING ON TRAVELING SAFELY

- *The Safe Travel Book, A Guide for the International Traveler,* Peter Savage, Revised Edition, Lexington, MA: Lexington Books, 1993, $12.95.
- *Travel Safely, Security Safeguards at Home and Abroad,* Jack Adler and Thomas C. Tompkins, New York, Hippocrene Books, 1988, $14.95.
- *The Business Travel Survival Guide,* Jack Cummings, New York: Wiley, 1991, $14.95.
- *The International Safe Travel Guide,* Robert C. Downes and William J. Bartman, Betterway, 1987. (available only in libraries, not book stores.)
- *A Safe Trip Abroad,* a brochure published by the Bureau of Consular Affairs, U.S. Department of State. Available from the Superintendent of Documents, U.S. Government Printing Office, P.O. Box 371954, Pittsburgh, PA 15250. (202)783-3238, $1.

CHAPTER 8

A CULTURAL SURVIVAL KIT

Lisa M. is an executive with a California manufacturer of computer chips. During a business trip to Japan, she found herself in a social setting one evening surrounded by a group of Japanese businessmen. She knew that Japanese businessmen unwind with after-hours drinking sessions, but she was totally unprepared for what happened next. Noticing her wedding ring, the men began asking questions about her husband: What did he think about her traveling overseas? Did they have children? Who took care of them while she was gone? These, Lisa thought, were perfectly natural questions. But then came the zingers: How much money do you make? How much is your house worth? And the clincher: What type of birth control pills do you take?

Relating this story after her return, Lisa shook her head and said, "I thought all Japanese were shy, quiet, and extremely polite. I was surprised and shocked by their questions. Was that normal behavior?"

We all carry mental baggage with us on trips overseas and it's packed into one powerful phrase: cultural stereotypes. Such things as:

- All Japanese are quiet, polite, and inscrutable.
- All Germans are stiff, punctual, and love beer.
- The French are rude, romantic, and proud.
- The English are aloof and conservative.
- Everyone in Latin America is either macho or late.
- Italians are loud, demonstrative, and like to pinch women's bottoms.

In Lisa's case, she assumed that all Japanese were too polite to ask questions that bordered on—by *her* standards—a clear invasion of her privacy. However, what she had encountered was normal, natural curiosity because, according to Japanese culture, married women never ventured abroad alone, especially in a business role.

COPING WITH CULTURAL DIFFERENCES

The best way to assure that your passage into these new cultural waters is smooth and enjoyable is to do a bit of homework prior to your departure. Fortunately, resources are plentiful. At the end of this chapter, you will find a list of various resources that deal with international behavior. You'll find more books at your local library or bookstore, especially about the specific country (or countries) you plan to visit.

Social behavior varies widely around the world. We have been conditioned to believe what's done in America is correct and proper everywhere. It's as though we view the world revolving on an axis driven straight down through the North American continent, and everything revolves around us. Academics call that "ethnocentrism," and it's natural for every social group to feel that way.

Rules for behavior vary from country to country. You won't necessarily be extradited for violating local rules of social behavior, but you'll enjoy your visit more if you are observant, aware, and even prepared for some of these differences.

For example, in our society, during social or business conversations, direct eye contact is considered important, even required. Yet in many Asian countries, parents teach their children to avoid direct eye contact of any kind because it is considered impolite.

To avoid making social gaffes and goofs in personal encounters while traveling abroad, we offer this general advice:

- Be sensitive and aware of the actions and behavior of others. When in doubt, ask a friend in that country, business associate, guide, or the concierge at your hotel.
- Always bear in mind that we are viewed as having peculiar behavior as well. For example, many Japanese consider the way we take a bath to be unhygienic. How can that be, you ask? Consider this. We draw the water, sit in it for a while, then soap up, wash off, and then soak again. Have you ever looked at that water? As Atlanta columnist Louis Grizzard says, "Never wash your face with something you've been sitting in." That's how the Japanese view us. The Japanese, on the other hand, take a bath before they take a bath: They enter one tub for a pre-soak; then step out to lather up with soap; then sponge off and enter a second bath to wash away the soap; and, finally, they enter a third bath reserved solely for soaking. Moral: In the eyes of others, we Americans do strange things.

BATHROOMS OF THE WORLD

The locale for daily and necessary bodily functions is provided around the world in a surprising number of different forms. So that you are fully prepared, here is a sampling of possible surprises you might encounter behind that universal door.

• In many countries, you won't even find a door. Along the autobahns of Germany, for example, you will probably spot a car or truck stopped along the side of the road with the driver or occupants standing facing the bushes along the road in that all-too-familiar posture.

• Also in France and other European countries, be prepared to find women bathroom attendants in the men's lavatories. In fact, in some buildings you may find unisex outer bathrooms (for washing the hands) with toilets in individual little roomettes for use by both sexes.

• In many European hotels and resorts, you will find an extra basin that is set lower. It's called a "bidet" and is used, especially in France, for bathing one's private parts. If you don't care to use it for bathing, it's an excellent washbasin for underwear and socks!

• Turning to more exotic locales (Japan and the Middle East come to mind), you might be directed to the door supposedly leading to the toilet, enter, and find what appears to be an empty room. Then your eyes will be drawn to a neat hole in the floor, fronted by two foot imprints etched into the wood or cement. Your brain quickly solves the riddle, and logic and a certain competitiveness in your spirit says, "Well, if they can hit that hole, so can I." After proving yourself correct, the first riddle is immediately followed by a second puzzle: No toilet tissue. Instead, there is a water spigot and, perhaps, a small vessel such as a metal pitcher. Once again, logic rises to the occasion along with a recollection that says "In the Middle East, one eats only with the right hand because the left hand is reserved for bodily hygiene." That's when you put all three elements—water, pitcher, left hand—into a logical equation that leads to your solution.

• When inquiring about the location of a bathroom, use the word "toilet" instead of any one the dozens of euphemisms we Americans enjoy so much, such as: restrooms, washroom, john, and so on. Avoid especially such highly confusing terms as "making a pit stop," U.S. military terminology (latrine and head), and the "boy's" or "girl's" room. One visitor to the Middle East kept asking about the "little boy's room" so often that his Arabic host finally inquired of his colleague, "Is it perhaps that your friend likes little boys?"

GREETINGS

Shaking hands, it is theorized, originated late in the Middle Ages to demonstrate that neither party was carrying a weapon in the right hand. And today, we continue to greet one another by clasping right hands. There are exceptions:

- Maori tribesmen in New Zealand greet one another by rubbing noses.
- Certain tribes in Central Africa spit at each other's feet as a greeting.
- In India and parts of Southeast Asia, people press their own palms together in a prayer-like gesture, and bow their heads slightly. This is called the "namaste" in India, and the "wai" in Thailand.
- And in Japan, they bow to one another. It is important to recognize that the bow is not considered an act of subservience; it is more an expression of respect and humility.

In most of Latin America, good friends (including male friends) will give an abrazo, or embrace. This involves a hearty bear hug, often with one hand clapping the other person's back. Incidentally, it is thought the body embrace originated centuries ago when people wore robes, therefore the embrace was also a method for checking the other person for weapons.

Good friends, including male friends, in places like Russia, France, Belgium, Italy, Spain, Portugal, and parts of the Middle East will also kiss cheeks. Usually, this is really just pressing cheeks while making a kissing sound, but in some of those locales a hearty smacker will actually be planted on the cheek.

In those countries influenced by the Latin culture, greetings involve more than just a handshake.

TRAVEL TIP   In Brazil, single women who are good friends will often kiss first one check, then the other, then back to the first, and then to the other again—four times in all. It has been said each kiss signifies a message: The first is merely a greeting; the second says "May you marry soon"; the third is "May you have children"; and the fourth says "And may your mother-in-law not come to live with you!" ∎

For more on this subject, please refer to Roger Axtell's book *Gestures: Do's and Taboos of Body Language Around the World* (Wiley, 1991).

DINING

As you venture overseas, be prepared for some sensational culinary delights—and possibly some gut-turning surprises as well.

The first change most Americans encounter is at breakfast. For example, in much of Europe, common breakfast fare often consists of cold cuts, hard rolls, cheese, coffee, or tea.

Each European country also seems to have a special favorite at breakfast: the French love their croissants; the English usually have eggs (soft boiled seem especially popular); and according to the National Honey Institute, over 80 percent of the people in Germany take honey at breakfast!

If you are staying in a large hotel any place in the world, they will probably cater to all tastes . . . including your favorite brand of cereal.

As for the mid-day meal, throughout Europe, Latin America, and much of the Far East, if you are being entertained by business associates or friends, what we may consider lunch is the main meal of the day. If you have difficulty downing a full three-course meal at noon, you can simply order two appetizers to supplant the first and second courses, and then politely skip the final course.

The evening meal may be, again, a full hot dinner, especially if you are being entertained. But for locals, dining in the evening at their own home is usually lighter fare. We, Americans, reverse this pattern: Light lunch, heavy dinner. The suggestion here is to be prepared to possibly reverse that habit.

Now, about what we eat: Most travelers expect to encounter new foods—indeed, some relish the idea of tasting reindeer meat in Norway, haggis in Scotland, new pastas in Italy, humous in the Middle East, exotic seafood in Southeast Asia, sushi in Japan, and Argentine steaks so tender you can literally cut them with a fork.

However, the first problem for most travelers comes when they open a menu . . . and find all those foreign words. How to translate in order to know what you're eating?

The obvious solutions are: Ask if a menu in English is available, or ask the waiter or maitre d' for either a verbal translation or for the specialties of the house. Even then, the most experienced travelers may be confronted with stomach-turning surprises.

Carol Salcito, travel executive and consultant, tells about the time she was in Singapore and decided that one item on the menu—"shrimp in liqueur"—sounded appetizing. Soon after, her waiter brought a covered dish, lifted the lid, and presented her with a huge mound of wiggling, live shrimp! Aghast, she turned to her dinner partner and stammered, "Would you like to try one of these first?" "My dear Carol," he responded, "the waiter is just demonstrating that your shrimp are fresh. He will return them to the kitchen to be cooked."

Other world travelers have not been as fortunate as Salcito. If you happen to be the guest of honor at a banquet in the Middle East, it is possible you will be served the delicacy of the menu: sheep's eyeballs . . . and you are expected to eat them.

In Mexico, visitors have been confronted with cooked insects such as chocolate covered ants. Milwaukee's Archbishop Weakland suggests you "just pretend they're pretzels."

What should you do when confronted with some strange, ugly-looking new food? As a tourist, you can always refuse unless you

You might encounter some strange foods overseas—try to enjoy them.

are venturesome (which is recommended). After all, people in that country have probably been eating it with impunity for centuries. On the other hand, if you are a guest-of-honor, to refuse, you risk offending your host or hostess. In that case, consider these solutions offered by several experienced world travelers:

- "Never ask 'What is this?' Just eat it."
- "Cut it up into thin slices and pretend it's chicken."
- "Swallow it quickly."

In summary, don't be afraid to try new and unusual foods. But, if in doubt, also don't be afraid to first ask, "What is the custom here?" That will save you the embarrassment of the American who was unfamiliar with the practice of serving finger bowls— and he drank his!

PUNCTUALITY

Different cultures view time in different ways. At the top of the chart are the time-conscious and highly punctual Scandinavians, Germans, and the Swiss. Americans, Canadians, other Northern Europeans—they all probably rank second in respecting and expecting punctuality. The Orient probably comes next on the scale, having been influenced perhaps by hordes of Western businesspeople who regard "time as money."

Next—nay, far down on the scale—come the inhabitants of Latin America. Almost to a person, time is considered something flexible, not rigid. They have adopted an attitude of "Why live one's life in measured segments?" There is one notable exception: In Spain it is proper to be on time for a bull fight.

Any American traveler leaving the boundaries of the United States would be wise to append one of two notes to his or her wristwatch. The first note, for destinations to any of those countries at the top of the "on time" list, should say "Be Punctual!" For those destinations on the lower half, your note should say, "Be Patient!"

GIFT GIVING

As a tourist, packing your bag does not usually require stockpiling gifts in one corner of your suitcase. Still, experienced travelers might stow away a small supply of small, portable gifts like pens, key chains, commemorative coins, or tokens from your city or state. These are handy for new friends acquired along the way or for the tour guide or concierge who goes beyond the normal line of duty.

Students who travel abroad can do the same, but may add such items as picture postcards of their home locales, T-shirts or baseball-style caps, and other souvenirs from their school or hometown.

TRAVEL TIP In at least one case, the cap idea backfired. One student traveling in Northern China passed out caps featuring the color of his school, which happened to be green. When he noticed that the recipients looked startled, he inquired and learned that in that region when men wear green hats it indicated their sisters were available for hired sex! ■

For business travelers, gift giving can be a more serious challenge. As a general rule, gift giving among business acquaintances is common in the Far East and the Middle East. There, cultures tend to be both especially gracious and generous.

TRAVEL TIP In the Middle East and Far East, avoid making gushing compliments over a painting that catches your fancy or a tea service that impresses you. Reason: You may be the recipient of it right on the spot. ■

In summary, gift giving when traveling abroad is not only more common, but it is more complex than here in the United States. The best advice is as follows:

- Try to do a bit of homework about the culture(s) you are visiting to see if they are big gift-givers and
- If in doubt, contact the Cultural Attaché at the embassy or nearest consulate for the country you plan to visit.

If you need further information on gift-giving abroad, see Roger Axtell's *Do's and Taboos Around the World*, 3rd Ed. (Wiley, 1993).

TIPPING

"To Insure Promptitude" is believed to be the origin of the word TIP. And while that seems sensible, the vexing questions of who to tip, when to tip, and how much to tip have plagued almost everyone who steps onto foreign soil.

The most comprehensive single guidebook we have encountered is *The International Guide to Tipping* by Nancy Star (Berkley

Books, 1988) (no longer available in book stores but available in some local libraries). This is a country-by-country guide to tipping and covers every conceivable handout from fishing boat captains to casino croupiers.

TRAVEL TIP As soon as you arrive in a foreign country, find a local friend (or a hotel concierge) and simply inquire: "Would you please tell me the proper guidelines for tipping here in your country?" Make certain you learn about the most common ones: taxi drivers, restaurant waiters, bell boys, doormen, and airport baggage handlers. And don't forget the concierge! As a general rule, tip the concierge for providing any special services (such as advice on tipping); and pay according to the magnitude of the service provided. For example, if he merely hands you the morning's complimentary newspaper, no tip is required. If, however, he suggests a good restaurant and makes table reservations for you, a tip of several dollars would be appropriate. But, be equally cautious about overtipping. Flashing $10 and $20 bills around is just as inappropriate as failing to tip. ■

TRAVEL TIP Always inquire "Are gratuities included?" This practice is often adopted in the United States for room service in hotels (and sometimes for all services at fine resorts), but it is much more common in Europe. There, you will find it practiced in hotels and restaurants. Therefore, when checking into a hotel, one of your first questions should be: Are gratuities included? That also solves your very first problem—whether to tip the bellboy. ■

TRAVEL TIP There are countries scattered around the globe where tipping is not customary. Iceland, The People's Republic of China, and Tahiti are three of those. Also, in certain key major cities the tip is automatically included in taxi fares. At last count, those cities included: Amsterdam, Athens, Bangkok, Brussels, Copenhagen, Geneva, Helsinki, Moscow, Oslo, Singapore, Tokyo, and Zurich. Don't bother trying to memorize these. Our best single piece of advice is *ask*. ■

Very Important Travel Tip. Use the smile liberally. It is not only universally understood, but it can help defuse unpleasant situations, help make new friends, and make you feel better . . . all with one simple gesture—the smile.

RECOMMENDED READING LIST

Specific book titles and other sources where more material can be obtained on this subject of preparing yourself for encountering new cultures include:

- *CULTURGRAMS* are short, four-page briefing papers on individual countries, one for each of about 100 nations. They provide specific information on customs, courtesies, lifestyle, and demographics for each country. Write to Publication Services, David M. Kennedy Center Publications, Brigham Young University, P.O. Box 24538, Provo, UT 84602-4538, (800)528-6279.
- The Intercultural Press Inc. publishes and distributes a wide assortment of books on cross-cultural matters. To obtain a catalog, write Intercultural Press Inc., P.O. Box 700, Yarmouth, ME 04096, (207)846-5168.
- *The Diplomat* monthly newsletter focuses on one country per issue, providing background information on international business practices and protocol. Each issue includes a general country overview, along with descriptions of dining customs, gift giving, holidays/festivals and travel hints. Annual subscription for $50 is available from The Diplomat, 31 Meadow Wood Drive, Greenwich, CT 06830, 203/869-1199. Single back issues are also available for $3 each.
- *Do's and Taboos Around the World, A Guide to International Behavior,* 3rd Ed., (Wiley, 1993), $12.95.
- *Gestures: Do's and Taboos of Body Language Around the World,* (Wiley, 1991), $9.95.
- *The Do's and Taboos of Hosting International Visitors,* (Wiley, 1990), $16.95.

CHAPTER 9

COPING WITH A FOREIGN LANGUAGE

Tom Cermola runs a travel bureau in San Diego. Tom says, "I travel to Europe frequently and early on in my travels I discovered that in places like Denmark and Germany, whenever I am introduced to someone and I say 'How do you do?' or 'How are you?', they don't know how to answer. I later learned that's because there is no equivalent salutation in their language. They just don't say that when they are introduced. And, when you stop and think about it, here in America if I am introduced to someone, say, at the supermarket, and I say 'How are you?', I really don't want to know! If they were to answer, 'Well, my back hurts a bit, and the dog got run over, and my mother's gout is kicking up . . .' I'd think they were crazy!"

Even though English can be a perplexing language for others, we are extremely fortunate because in every corner of the world it is possible to find someone who speaks English. In fact, English is either the official or unofficial language in some 59 countries and studied in another 51.

That's the good news. The bad news is that we've messed up our language with idioms, jargon, buzz words, euphemisms, slang, acronyms, and military and sports terminology—plus innocent-sounding pleasantries like "How do you do?"

Other than our frequent use of jargon, there are three other complaints about Americans:

- We're often accused of speaking much too fast.
- Our humor is too often based on a play on words.
- We Americans are notoriously monolingual.

As a result, when we travel abroad it is like traveling on a communications unicycle—with only one form of verbal locomotion.

How do we cope? Sally Wecksler, a literary agent who works with dozens of foreign language publishers, says, "Americans seem to think if they can't speak another language they should just speak louder. We must realize that people with foreign accents are not hard of hearing."

Many people around the world have learned British English, which can differ dramatically from American English in both pronunciation and usage.

People with foreign accents are *not* hard of hearing.

It's important to recognize that American English has definite limitations and it would be a good investment of time—plus a few dollars, perhaps—to consider learning a few foreign language words and phrases.

HOW TO COMMUNICATE EFFECTIVELY

The following seven tips will help you communicate effectively. Follow these suggestions and it could mean the difference between an enjoyable trip abroad and a prolonged travel nightmare.

1. Speak slowly and distinctly. Among international business savants, it is said you can determine who the experienced professionals are by the slow pace of their speech.
2. Avoid all of the following:
   - Idioms ("It's raining cats and dogs.")
   - Slang ("We don't want any hanky panky with this business deal.")
   - Euphemisms ("I need to visit the restroom.")
   - Sports terminology ("When in doubt drop back and punt.")

- Acronyms ("We need a reservation ASAP.")
- Jargon ("My PC takes CD-ROM programs.")

Speak and write using simple syntax, word choice, and vocabulary.

3. Watch the eyes. In fact, watch for all types of body language. Social scientists claim that fully 60 percent of our daily communication is nonverbal. But the eyes are especially important. Among some cultures, it is believed "the eyes are the windows of the soul." And when trying to communicate, a person's eyes will tell you much about comprehension. (*Note:* The exception is among Oriental cultures where direct eye contact is considered impolite.)

4. Repeat numbers, or write them down for all to see. In the Japanese language, for instance, numbers are stated in a different form. For example, in Japanese one million is stated as "one-hundred, ten thousands." Even without those differences, when crossing back and forth between languages, it is easy to become confused.

5. Never assume that people around you do not understand English. For instance, it's tempting, when in a public setting, such as riding on public transportation, to assume that because you do not hear any English, your fellow passengers do not comprehend it. In situations like this, Americans are often guilty of making critical remarks about the locale, the conveyance, or even the people. However, it is entirely possible that someone within earshot is fully fluent in English. This is one of those occasions where the label "ugly American" would justifiably apply.

6. Learn some phrases in the language of the country you plan to visit. We Americans are impressed and grateful when international visitors come to our country, and they have taken the time and effort to learn at least a few words in English. Empathy and goodwill develop and both host and guest begin to construct a bond of friendship.

7. British English is different in thousands of ways from American English. Throughout those countries that once comprised the British Empire, residents learned the "mother tongue." We in the United States adopted English as our official language (although it was selected only after a narrow victory over German), and then created our own special dialect, which is properly called American English.

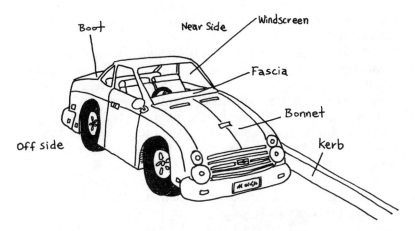

The same word can have different meanings around the world, as in England where automobile parts are described differently than in the United States.

"Two nations separated by a common language." That well-known quotation is attributed to the great Irish writer George Bernard Shaw, and the truth of Shaw's observation has been documented over and over again.

TRAVEL TIP If you plan to drive an automobile in Great Britain, be prepared for some significant differences in terminology. In fact, there are at least 60 different labels. Here are some examples: an American dashboard is called the "fascia" by the British, the windshield is the "windscreen," the trunk is the "boot," the hood is the "bonnet," and the fenders are called "wings." Even the two sides of a car have different names: In America we refer to the "driver's side" and the "passenger side." In the United Kingdom, the left side is referred to as the "nearside," because in a country where all driving is done on the left side of the road, it is nearest the curb (spelled "kerb" in England). The driver's, or right, side of a car is called the "offside." Conclusion: If you plan to rent a car (called "hiring a car" in England), it is helpful to know that these differences exist, and to try to learn a bit of this new vocabulary. ◼

Much of British English terminology applies if you visit Australia, New Zealand, South Africa, or other countries where the British people influenced early traditions and customs. However, even among those former British colonies, a special vocabulary has evolved.

The Australian Tourist Commission provides *A Fair Dinkum Aussie Dictionary* with over 300 words that are unique to their country. For example, "Fair Dinkum" means "true, genuine; an assertion of truth or genuineness, as in the statement, 'It's true, mate, fair dinkum.'" To learn more about Australia, contact the Tourist Commission at (800)333-0199; inquiries about the dictionary should be made at the Australian Tourist Offices in New York, (212)687-6300 or Los Angeles, (310)552-1988.

For anyone with a deeper interest in the subject of differences between American English and British English, here are two good reference books:

1. *The British/American Language Dictionary* by Norman Moss (Passport Books, 1984), $8.95.
2. *Understanding British English* by Margaret E. Moore (Carol Publishing Group, 1992), $9.95.

LEARNING SOME FOREIGN PHRASES

A few hours invested in learning key phrases in another language can make a world of difference in enjoying your trip abroad. Your local library and bookstores have a wide selection of learning aids.

For example, just knowing the words for bathroom, hotel, church, airport, hospital, office, restaurant, room, bank, and market can make the difference between success and frustration in a single day. Then add words like please, thank you, good morning, good afternoon, and essential question-oriented words like where, when, what, why, and how, and you can turn the total darkness of ignorance into at least a glimmer of comprehension.

In the foregoing paragraph are listed less than 20 key words. How long would it take you to learn those words in French, or Spanish, or even Japanese? An hour? Less? Your trip could be significantly enhanced by devoting that hour to some simple exercises in memorization.

The starting place is, once again, our old friends your public library or neighborhood bookstores where language learning aids abound. For the more serious student, it might pay to purchase a few cassettes, which are freely available at most any bookstore or by mail order. Following are a few such programs, which can be ordered through the Book Passage mail-order bookstore at (800)321-9785.

- *LANGUAGE/30.* This teaching system offers 30 different languages taught via a self-learning method. The learning system is based on the U.S. military "speed-up" language learning method developed for U.S. government personnel preparing for overseas duty. The course is comprised of two audio cassettes, a phrase dictionary, and a handy carrying case. Conversational and useful words and phrases are stressed.
- *Berlitz Language Cassettepaks.* These classic language sets combine a 60-minute learning tape with a color-coded phrasebook. Included are thousands of phrases and words, useful for shopping, eating and getting around.
- The *AUDIO-FORUM Language Courses.* Developed by the Foreign Service Institute for diplomats who must learn a language in a hurry, these cassettes and booklets emphasize speaking and understanding rather than rote learning.
- *Just Listen and Learn.* For learning the basics, this system offers a coursebook and three one-hour cassettes. For those with a foundation in a particular language who want to brush up, consider the *Practice and Improve* cassettes and workbooks issued by the same source.
- *Language Tapes for Children.* These are designed as introductions for kids with many illustrations. Tapes deal with subjects like counting, greetings and socializing.

CHAPTER 10

BUSINESS TRIPS

Dean A. owns a successful construction equipment firm in the United States. He recently returned from his first business trip abroad and said, "I plead guilty! I decided to head for Europe to chase up some business and found I was totally unprepared for what I encountered. I started by phoning potential customers for appointments and was given the cold shoulder: I was asked for my SIC number—whatever that was. I was asked if I qualified under something called ISO 9000, and had to tell them I didn't know. When I was asked who my distributor was, I had to confess I didn't have one. And finally, I never realized how jet lag could knock you for such a loop. Next time I'm going to do better homework before I leave."

Dean had overlooked a time-honored motto of business as well as of the Boy Scouts: "Be prepared." This chapter provides a primer on how to prepare for a business trip abroad.

THE ROLE OF THE U.S. DEPARTMENT OF COMMERCE

Start by contacting your nearest District Office of the U.S. Department of Commerce. Offices are located in every major U.S. city, and within each of those offices you will find staff of the Department's International Trade Administration (ITA). People in that bureau are there for the specific purpose of helping you walk through the paces toward finding business overseas.

For example, they will determine the S.I.C. number that mystified our friend Dean. That stands for Standard Industrial Classification, and it is merely a gigantic international numbering system that assigns code numbers to each and every type of manufactured product.

At those ITA offices, trained trade specialists will acquaint you with a host of services provided by the federal government. For example, they can provide valuable statistical data in countries where your product or service might be needed. They will even provide you with a list of potential distributors for your product in various countries.

The ISO 9000 term that Dean A. encountered is simply a code name for a system adopted by the European Common Market for establishing quality and other standards in order to have your product accepted in the countries comprising that Common Market.

People at those offices will also eliminate other bugaboos that bedevil new-to-export businesspeople. For example, for businesspeople who don't want to get paid in pesos or francs, the solution is simple: U.S. banks with international divisions will explain how almost all U.S. exporters get paid, safely and securely, in U.S. dollars through a banking instrument called a "letter of credit."

Service firms throughout the United States called "freight forwarders" are well experienced in helping exporters pack, ship, and insure shipments being sent anywhere in the world.

The U.S. Department of Commerce can help you prepare for your first business trip abroad.

The ITA people will also supply you with names of firms in the United States called Export Management Companies (EMCs) that will serve as your total export department, perhaps saving you the time and expense of establishing your own department.

The ITA will help you decide if your first foray into the international marketplace should be through a trade show. This is one of the most popular ways for newcomer companies to establish business contacts overseas. The ITA maintains a detailed schedule of trade shows, by business category, all over the world. At such a trade show, you can mix and meet with scores of potential business contacts and shop the competition as well.

Another resource for help may be from your state government. At this writing, 44 states are operating a total of 163 foreign trade offices in 25 countries overseas. Check with your state's Department of Commerce and Development to see what services they provide.

If you are still unpersuaded, consider that your federal and state tax dollars are providing these services for one purpose: To help you do business overseas.

TRAVEL TIP Obtain a copy of the Commerce Department publication titled *A Basic Guide to Exporting.* This comprehensive guide provides valuable information on everything from developing a marketing plan to providing a glossary of terms used in international trade. To order a copy, call the Government Printing Office at (202)783-3238 and ask for stock number 003-009-00604-0. The cost is $9.50. ■

Now that you have been introduced to the most important starting points for doing business abroad, let's examine 16 specific tricks and tips for preparing for your business trip.

TIPS FOR PREPARING A BUSINESS TRIP ABROAD

1. Order an extra supply of business cards. The reason is that you will be passing them out like candy to children, especially if you are attending a trade show. Business cards are freely exchanged in international commerce.
2. Arrange all business appointments well in advance. Set up your appointments weeks and months in advance and have them confirmed in writing. Unlike Americans, businesspeople overseas do not check into a hotel and start making telephone calls for appointments. In fact, the American proclivity for conducting business by phone is not as common overseas. That is probably the reason Dean A. received the cold shoulder.
3. School yourself on how to economically and effectively phone and fax back to the United States from wherever you are overseas. (Also see Chapter 4.)
4. As you begin to develop your timetable and itinerary for your trip overseas, ask ITA staff members for its list of national and religious

Be sure to carry an *extra* supply of business cards on every trip.

holidays around the world. You won't be able to conduct business on a day, or during a period, when a country is celebrating a holiday.

5. Arm yourself with the U.S. State Department's *Background Notes* for each country you plan to visit. These are chock full of information on the history, form of government, economics, demographics, and other helpful information. Copies may be available to study or copy at your local library, or they can be obtained by contacting The Superintendent of Documents, U.S. Government Printing Office, P.O. Box 371954, Pittsburg, PA 15250, (202)783-3238.

6. Keep a daily journal. Experienced world travelers often carry small, shirt pocket-sized notebooks—one for each country on their itinerary. These are handy to record daily expenses, names and addresses to remember, jottings about things to do when returning home, foreign phrases to remember, and bits and pieces of personal information gleaned from new business contacts. Business travelers record all types of thoughts and impressions in these little notebooks, the reason being that when traveling to several countries on a single trip, it is easy to confuse happenings and experiences. These little journals then become invaluable on the next visit to that country.

7. Work closely with your travel agent to lay out a complete itinerary, along with ground transportation to and from your hotel. If at all possible, fly business class to any destination that requires more than four hours flying time. The need to arrive as fresh and rested as possible is especially important in business.

   You may also want to consider hiring a car and driver in the cities you are visiting (see Chapter 2), especially if you have numerous appointments. Be certain the travel agent acquaints you with all requirements concerning your passport, visas, and vaccinations.

8. Study the remedies for jet lag suggested in Chapter 6. Most business travelers will testify that jet lag can be one of the most insidious disruptions of clear thinking and top performance.

9. Investigate the ATA Carnet system if you are planning to carry along commercial samples, advertising material, audiovisual material, medical or scientific equipment, or other

tools of your trade. The United States is a member of this system, which permits business travelers to carry these materials into a country for temporary periods without paying duties, taxes, or posting a bond.

Contact the U.S. Council of International Business, 1212 Avenue of the Americas, New York, NY 10036, (212)354-4480, for a list of member countries within the Carnet system and the schedule of fees required.

10. Dress conservatively. Well-tailored clothes in good fabrics are the safest rule for men and women when conducting business almost any place in the world. That means dark-colored suits and dresses with subdued patterns, white or muted shirts or blouses, and conservative accessories.

11. Consider Canada first when seeking to expand outside the United States. It is already the United States's largest trading partner, and we share the longest, friendliest border in the world.

12. Consider stowing away a few general purpose gifts. See Chapter 8 for some tips on giving gifts.

13. Read Chapters 6 and 7 on the subjects of health and safety since both are extremely important when traveling on business.

14. Write two types of letters upon your return home to contacts you have made overseas: (1) Thank you notes for people who assisted or hosted you and (2) letters of confirmation to cover any agreements or general understandings you made.

15. Have any sales literature and price lists you plan to carry and distribute translated into the local language before you leave home. The same is true for weights and measurements, since the metric system prevails in almost every other section of the world except the United States.

16. Take along an extra portion of patience when you pack your briefcase. Doing business overseas usually takes more time than expected.

RECOMMENDED READING

- *The Business Travel Survival Guide,* by Jack Cummings (Wiley, 1991), $14.95. While much of the advice in this book pertains to the businessperson traveling in the United States, there are also segments and tips for the international traveler. Cummings has divided this helpful book into logical and very readable sections interspersed with specific tips. While any type of traveler will find Cummings' advice useful, this book is especially appropriate for the business traveler. Cummings has for 20 years owned and operated an international travel agency that specializes in business travel, personally logs over 300,000 miles of travel each year, and is the author of 10 nonfiction books. Look in the "Travel" section of your library or bookstore for this book.

- *The International Business Traveler's Companion,* by Donald E. deKieffer, $17.95, is published by the Intercultural Press (P.O. Box 700, Yarmouth, ME 04096, (207)846-5168. This book, written with the business traveler in mind, provides both a checklist in preparation for a trip plus chapters on each of the major issues a business traveler might face: eating, drinking, entertaining, traveling with the family, and how to plug into local business processes and practices.

CHAPTER 11

INSURANCE

Jeff and Phillip arrived at the international terminal for O'Hare Airport at the prescribed two hours before their flight departed, checked their luggage, and picked up some reading material. Jeff then said "I've got to buy some flight insurance coverage, too." Phil looked surprised, saying "Why? I've got my life insurance, and a household umbrella policy to cover other losses. Besides, air travel is safer than driving down the highway." Jeff objected, "Not for me. I've got every type of insurance coverage possible—trip cancellation, accident and sickness, baggage loss. The whole works."

Who was correct? Jeff or Phil? Actually, travel insurance is a personal decision, but travelers can insure themselves to cover every contingency. For instance, you can actually obtain insurance against jury duty, or for a 24-hour period without luggage, or even if you should abruptly and without any special reason change your mind after buying an airline ticket.

We will examine the seven basic categories of travel insurance.

TYPES OF INSURANCE

1. Flight insurance to cover death and injury in the event of a crash, collision, fire, or other serious mishap.
2. Baggage and personal effects insurance, to cover damage or loss.
3. Trip cancellation and interruption insurance, which applies mainly to charter and packaged tour trips.
4. Default or bankruptcy insurance; this usually applies if and when airlines or tour operators go belly up during your long-planned vacation trip.
5. Automobile insurance, to cover driving a rented car or your own car while outside the country.
6. Personal accident and sickness insurance, in case either occurs while out of the United States.
7. Combination policies.

Now let's examine each basic category of insurance and learn the details.

Flight Insurance.   Flight insurance can be obtained from some local insurance agents, from some travel agencies, and from insurance sales counters at most major airports.

Flight insurance usually covers you from the moment you step on to the airport premises. It covers:

- Regularly scheduled flights;
- When your flight is substituted with a land or water conveyance vehicle provided by the airline;
- When you are being transported to and from your insured form of travel (taxi, bus limousine, etc.); and
- Some companies also insure you on certain military carriers.

The first step is to check your current life policies for accidental death or injury. Many life policies are written with "double indemnity" or twice the death benefit for accidental death. Also, your employer may provide death benefit coverage that can apply outside your employment.

Many travel writers warn about purchasing insurance at airports, either from service counters or vending machines. The first reason is that airline travel is among the safest of all forms of travel. Secondly, flight insurance is among the most expensive forms of life insurance coverage you can buy. Also, some credit cards provide free flight insurance if you pay for your ticket using that credit card.

Here is a sampling of cost and benefits taken from a major national insurance company:

- Cost was 25¢ per $7,500 of the principal sum selected.
- Benefits are paid for "accidental loss of life, limb, or sight within 100 days of a covered accident."
- The principal sum (meaning the amount you buy) is paid in the event of loss of life, two limbs, two eyes, or one limb and one eye.
- Some medical expenses are also covered.

But even this randomly picked application form had some "fine print" or exclusion provisions. For example, you were not covered if you were a nonfare passenger in California, implying that if you were using a free ticket in that state, you wouldn't be covered.

Insurance for Baggage and Personal Effects.   Before buying additional insurance to cover lost or stolen luggage, check your personal insurance coverage to see if your homeowner's policy covers this type of loss. If not, one option is to purchase a special "floater," which then provides you with such coverage.

Before you pay extra money for this type of insurance, you should know that if an airline loses your baggage, U.S. carriers are required to pay up to $1,250 per passenger. On international flights, the weight of the luggage determines the amount of reimbursement, although the maximum payment is about $635 per piece of checked baggage.

If you wish to have more coverage, you can buy "excess baggage" insurance from either a travel insurance firm or from the airline. This type of policy currently costs $1 to $2 per $100 worth of coverage, up to a maximum of $5,000.

You should also be aware of a practice called "primary coverage." That means if you buy additional insurance from an airline or travel insurance firm, they may pay you but then they will go to your personal homeowner's insurance company and collect from them.

Your homeowner's policy may provide protection, but most policies have a deductible amounting to $100 or more, so you usually don't collect the full amount of your loss.

As always, read the exclusions in any policy. In the case of lost luggage, some policies exclude such things as cash, tickets, furs, gold, and silver, art, and antiques. Some insurance companies reimburse only the depreciated value of the lost articles. The best way to establish the value of personal items (cameras, laptop computers, radios, etc.) is to have receipts and records of serial numbers and, for expensive items, to insure for an appraised amount.

A list of companies that offer various types of travel insurance—including insurance for lost or stolen bags—can be found at the end of this chapter.

If, during your trip, your luggage is not delivered to you, go immediately to the baggage claim office of your airline and file a lost luggage report. Odds are very good your luggage will be located and returned to you—eventually.

Trip Cancellation and Interruption Insurance.   The consensus of many travel writers is that whenever you are putting up big sums of money in advance for such things as charters, cruises, or package tours, it is wise to consider buying this type of insurance coverage.

If you must unexpectedly cancel or fail to complete a scheduled trip, or if the travel supplier fails to fulfill its obligation, you risk losing the money you advanced.

Travelers have been stranded in a distant city because their tour operator or chartered airline declared bankruptcy. Cruise company bankruptcies are less frequent, but when they do happen the Federal Maritime Commission requires ships that depart from U.S. ports to post large bonds to protect passengers. Cruises leaving from foreign ports, however, do not have such coverage.

Trip cancellation insurance usually applies if and when a doctor-verified injury or illness, a death in the family, or other unforeseen circumstances (e.g., extreme weather, a traffic accident, verifiable traffic delays) causes you to miss or cancel a trip. Some policies may offer protection if the illness or death of your travel partner occurs, forcing you to cancel or return home prematurely.

Costs vary and you should obtain quotes from several different sources, but as an example, a fee of $60 per $1,000 might be charged. If you decide to buy this type of insurance, do so at the same time you make advance payments for the trip or tour itself.

When determining how much interruption insurance coverage to buy, consider the following: The cost of returning home from your farthest destination at economy rates, which might be considerably higher than the chartered tour fare you paid originally; also, cost of living expenses should you be delayed in returning.

When purchasing any of these policies, ask about stipulations concerning family members and "pre-existing medical conditions."

Automobile Insurance.   Any traveler who has ever rented a car is confronted with the dilemma of "Should I, or shouldn't I, sign up for extra insurance?"

When renting a car in any country overseas, the following considerations are important:

• First, check with your insurer in this country to learn what coverage follows you when you drive outside the United States. Ask what to do about repairs and costs incurred overseas, and how you will be reimbursed. It's a good idea to get this in writing from your insurance company.

• Second, it's usually best to rent your car before you leave through a travel agent. That way, you know the rates and conditions, a car is reserved and ready for you when you arrive, and you can consider and decide in advance what type of insurance coverage is best for you.

TRAVEL TIP   If you will be driving from one country to another, make certain your rental contract allows you to take the car across borders, and that any insurance policy you purchase covers you in every country you plan to visit. ■

• In Europe, whether you drive your own or a rental car, you must carry public liability and property damage (third-party) insurance. It is compulsory. Therefore, car rentals in Europe usually include public liability, property damage, fire and theft coverage. Often they will also include collision damage coverage with a deductible provision.

• In a typical car rental contract, you can buy optional collision damage waiver (CDW) protection. Costs range from $6 to $15 a day, depending on the country. If you don't buy CDW coverage, you may be liable for as much as the full retail value of the rental car. Once again, however, check with your insurance agent in the United States to see if you are already covered when driving overseas. The same applies to credit card companies, some of whom provide insurance for rental cars; however, it may be that some overseas-based car rental companies will not honor insurance provided by credit cards. U.S.-based rental car companies will likely honor the insurance you get through your credit card.

• When driving a car in Europe, you must carry an International Insurance Certificate (or "Green Card"), which you can obtain from your local insurance broker in the United States. This certificate is valid throughout Europe, except for those countries that comprised the former Soviet Union. For information on insurance companies in those countries, contact Intourist-USA, Inc., 610 Fifth Ave., Suite 603, New York, NY 10020, (212)757-3884.

Personal Accident and Sickness Insurance.   The first piece of information to know is this: What does your current medical/ dental insurance coverage provide if you become ill or injured while traveling outside the United States? You should know the answer(s) in order to judge what more—if any—is required.

For example, Medicare and Medicaid cover you only in North America. Most Blue Cross/Blue Shield or U.S. Healthcare plans will only cover emergency care while overseas. Canadians are usually protected under their home province insurance plans.

A great number of American travelers with U.S. private or employer-provided health insurance coverage are protected when traveling abroad. And in most of those cases, they need only produce documents and receipts for expenses incurred for treatment while overseas to be reimbursed for medical-related expenses.

However, the problem occurs when you become ill overseas and you're confronted with a situation where the hospital demands a large payment or deposit, perhaps even before doing tests or performing surgery.

A Wisconsin woman faced just such an acute situation while vacationing in Italy. Doctors recommended immediate surgery and even though she had purchased extra travel and medical insurance, the hospital demanded $2,500 in advance. She had U.S. dollar traveler's checks, but the hospital refused to accept them. It was a weekend so the banks were closed, and she couldn't get the checks cashed. The hospital agreed to take her Visa credit card but with other travel expenses up to that point, she was near her limit. She frantically called a friend back in the United States who deposited $10,000 in her Visa account. Only then did the hospital proceed. She had tried to phone her insurance company about advancing money to the hospital, but due to a breakdown in communications, the hospital claimed it had not been contacted. Cost for one week in the hospital exceeded $10,000 and, in time, all claims were paid.

Experiences like this suggest that wise travelers should have extra sources for quick cash emergency loans back home. One method would be to obtain a larger line of credit with your credit card company.

It is worth researching companies that specialize in providing medical insurance while abroad. Write to a half-dozen of them (as we did in preparing this section), and you will soon discover that a wide range of services are available—everything from guaranteeing hospital deposits to paying for your corpse to be "repatriated." As with most things in life, however, these wide-ranging services are available for a price.

Here is a sampling of the types of services offered by a handful of national companies specializing in worldwide travel and health insurance:

- Hospital services;
- Outpatient services;
- Prescription medicines;
- Physician charges;
- Lab fees and x-rays;

- Local ambulance transportation;
- Emergency evacuation (to a nearby hospital or even to your home hospital if medically required);
- 24-hour telephone assistance services (multilingual staff to help locate nearest medical assistance, help with replacement of lost documents, help arrange for legal representation, etc.); and
- In the event of death, repatriation of remains.

Some companies will even arrange to send a doctor or specialist to your location overseas to personally evaluate your condition. They will also pay the transportation costs for a family member to join you overseas if and when you are hospitalized for more than seven days while traveling by yourself.

If you are traveling on business, check with your employer about Workers' Compensation coverage.

The range of services available is extensive. One company offers no less than 40 such emergency medical services. Note that all of these insurance programs have sections titled "Exclusions and Limitations." For example, eyeglasses, contact lenses, hearing aids, and dental care might be excluded. Alternately, any injury related to mountaineering might be excluded. Read the limitations section carefully.

There is no shortage of either types of coverage or number of companies offering this type of insurance. Your job will be to decide what type of coverage you need or want over and above your current medical insurance coverage, and to decide how much you are willing to pay for this extra coverage.

Combination Policies. Just as this term implies, these are policies that provide insurance coverage for several or all of the categories described previously. These combination packages are offered for either an individual or for families. Costs are calculated according to which options you choose from the categories listed in this chapter, and the duration of your trip.

Combination insurance packages are also available for the type of trip you may be taking. For example, a combination insurance policy is available and tailored just for cruises.

HOW POLICIES CAN BE OBTAINED

1. Purchasing one-time short-term policies;
2. Through clauses or riders on conventional, existing policies such as your homeowner's policy;
3. Through benefits provided by travel clubs or credit cards;

4. Through special insurance programs provided for the frequent traveler; and
5. Through combination policies sold by insurance agents, auto clubs, travel agents, or tour operators.

WHERE TO START

• Phone your own insurance agent or broker. Explain your plans and ask what type of insurance coverage your current policies provide for any of the situations described earlier. Odds are that your auto and homeowner's policies will provide partial coverage for some types of losses and accidents, but it's unlikely that you will be fully protected for all types of mishaps.

• Phone your medical insurance provider. Be sure to explain that you will be traveling outside the United States. Ask if there are limitations to your medical coverage when you are abroad. Also ask if there are special steps required if you become ill while overseas, incur expenses, and then wish to file claims for repayment. The same procedure applies if you have dental insurance.

Whether you're driving or walking, protecting yourself in some overseas cities is a must.

- Ask your local insurance agent what types of additional travel coverage he or she offers, for what durations of time, and the various costs.
- Check to see if any of your credit cards offer travel insurance as a free, automatic service of holding that card.

TRAVEL TIP Read the fine print in each and every policy! For example, travel writer Christopher Reynolds cites one policy that covers you "if you are a victim of unannounced strikes or civil commotion that affects public transportation. But, if your losses are associated with acts of war or insurrections or hostilities, whether or not war is declared, you wouldn't be covered." Who decides when civil commotion has become an insurrection? The insurers. ■

In summary, before you buy additional insurance for your next trip abroad, you need to know where you will be going, what you will be doing (e.g., skiing, driving, scuba diving, mountain climbing), what you will be taking with you (especially in the way of jewelry and other valuables), and what insurance coverage you have under existing policies.

INSURANCE COMPANIES

A listing of companies that offer the types of insurance services described in this chapter follows. (*Note:* Inclusion in this list does not imply recommendation or endorsement of services offered; the listings are provided merely as a service to the reader. The prospective traveler should examine each on its own merits, while seeking additional advice from local insurance agents and counselors.)

- Access America, P.O. Box 90315, Richmond, VA 23286-4991, (800)284-8300, offers all types of insurance protection and 24-hour help for travel in North America, overseas, and aboard cruise ships.
- Carefree Travel Insurance, P.O. Box 310, 120 Mineola Blvd., Mineola, NY 11501, (516)294-0220 or (800)323-3149, provides coverage for emergency medical evacuation and accidental death and dismemberment, plus 24-hour medical phone advice.
- International SOS Assistance, P.O. Box 11568, Philadelphia, PA 19116, (215)244-1500 or (800)523-8930, is a medical assistance company providing emergency evacuation services worldwide, medical referrals, and optional medical insurance.

- Travel Guard International, underwritten by Transamerica Occidental Life Companies, 1145 Clark St., Stevens Point, WI 54481, (715)345-0505 or (800)782-5151, offers reimbursement for medical expenses with no deductibles or daily limits, and emergency evacuation services. This company also offers bankruptcy/default protection and cancellation/interruption insurance.
- Wallach and Company, Inc., P.O. Box 480, Middleburg, VA 22117-0480, (703)687-3166 or (800)237-6615, offers comprehensive medical coverage, including emergency evacuation services worldwide.
- Travel Assistance International (provided by Worldwide Assistance Services, Inc.), 1133 15th Street, N.W., Suite 400, Washington, DC 20005, (202)331-1609 or (800)821-2828, provides comprehensive programs for medical, trip cancellation/disruption, and baggage loss. Also provides personal assistance in locating attorneys, interpreters, lost luggage or documents, and in making emergency travel arrangements.
- NEAR, Near Services, International Corporate Headquarters, 450 Prairie, Suite 101, Calumet City, IL 60409, (708)868-6700 or (800)654-6700, provides combination insurance coverage.

12

LUGGAGE AND PACKING

History shows that it wasn't the Russians who defeated Napoleon in 1812—it was the amount of baggage he took to Moscow. So says writer Kenneth R. Morgan, who adds that, with suitcases, "two is company, three's a crowd, and four will drive you to defeat."

For many travelers, one of the least enjoyable prospects about world travel is packing. On the eve of every trip, each of us asks those fateful questions: What should I pack? How can I pack it all efficiently. What do I do if I'm separated from my luggage?

In this chapter, we offer answers to those challenging questions. Let's begin by examining the matter of luggage, and specifically how to make your choice of baggage a less weighty burden.

WHICH TYPE OF LUGGAGE IS BEST?

That question has as many favorite answers as there are types of luggage. Every experienced traveler has his or her own opinion about which is best: Soft-sided? Hard-sided? Suit bags? With wheels? Without wheels? With "pull" handles or without? Expensive or cheap?

Here is a sampling from the gamut of opinions:

- Soft-sided luggage is best because it expands and therefore allows me to cram and cram and cram; empty, it's also lighter in weight.
- Hard-sided luggage is best because it protects my belongings better. Fragile items are less prone to breakage. Also, if caught in the rain, hard-sided luggage won't leak like soft-sided stuff often does.
- Garment or suit-bags are better because they keep my clothes wrinkle-free, and I can merely hang the complete bag in my hotel closet.
- Luggage fitted with wheels allows me to walk easily through airports without straining my back.
- Wheels always get knocked off and I end up with a lopsided case. Worse yet, they get jammed and won't roll and I have to pull them along like I'm tugging on a donkey.

- I never buy expensive luggage because it gets such rough treatment; it also invites theft.
- I never buy cheap luggage because it falls apart so easily and my clothes come tumbling out.

Each of these statements has some merit. And each type of luggage has its partisan following. If you are in doubt, here's a tip, especially if you favor carry-on luggage:

TRAVEL TIP Watch what the flight crews and attendants use. For example, they were the first to adopt the new, ruggedly constructed cases with built-in, padded handles and good-sized wheels. Also, the extendable handle serves the double purpose of allowing "piggybacking" of other pieces of luggage. ■

Carry-on luggage comes in many forms: duffel bags, tote bags, suit bags, backpacks or rucksacks, attache, and briefcases. Air passengers are allowed one carry-on piece of luggage that must fit in either the overhead compartments or under the seat in front of you. In the United States in 1987, the FAA ruled that all airlines must regulate the size and number of bags passengers may carry aboard an airplane. Regulations may vary according to the size of the aircraft. One fairly common set of measurements for European aircraft is that carry-on bags must measure no more than 18 inches by 14 inches by 6 inches (or in centimeters, 45 cm by 35 cm by 150 cm).

Other items you may carry aboard in addition to the one allowed piece include a (ladies) handbag, an overcoat, an umbrella or walking stick, a small camera, a pair of binoculars, an infant's food for the flight, a carrying basket for infants, a handicapped person's fully collapsible wheelchair, a pair of crutches, reading material (in reasonable quantities), and any duty-free goods you have acquired since checking-in for the flight.

TRAVEL TIP If you have never purchased duty-free items at an airport, it works like this. You make your selection at the duty-free shop in or near the airport; you pay for the item and receive a receipt. The actual merchandise is not delivered to you until you reach the gate for entering your airplane. In fact, some duty-free merchandise is not handed over to you until you reach the actual door of the airplane. You must show your receipt to the attendant in order to claim the merchandise. ■

As for checked luggage, some airlines have eliminated the weight allowance in favor of a limit of two pieces. (Depending on the airline, golf clubs and skis may be counted within that limit.) The limit on the size of a piece of luggage is a combined 62 inches (that's length plus width plus height), weighing no more than 70 pounds. Since some charter flights may have special restrictions, if you have any concerns, check with your travel agent for details before departure. As a general rule, it's always wise to check with your travel agent about all possible baggage restrictions.

Cruise ships and railroads customarily have no restrictions on size, weight, or number of bags.

Here are some things to look for when buying any type of luggage:

- Check zippers to assure they are the large "industrial," rugged type, with large and secure pull tabs. Cheap leather or plastic pull tabs have shorter lives.
- Handles should be equally rugged and affixed in the strongest possible ways, with heavy-duty rivets and stitching.
- Corners and edges should be protected since they receive the heaviest wear and tear when tossed from conveyors to luggage carts and vice versa. If the framework is made of metal, such as magnesium, make sure it is sturdy enough to withstand airport torture tests.
- Hang-up hooks should have a heavy-duty chain and always have two features: a coating of plastic on the hook itself for protection, and a method of fastening or tucking the hook inside the bag to avoid flailing around and becoming a danger to you and others.

If you favor soft-sized luggage, make certain it is water-repellent and made of ultra-tough 1,000-denier nylon to resist tears and punctures. (Denier is a unit of fineness for synthetic fabrics, and the higher the denier count, the better.) One authority recommends a minimum of 400-denier for luggage.

Lightness is the newest byword in luggage. Suitcases no longer must be built with the heft of Captain Hook's treasure chest. Manufacturers have been successful in recent years in crafting featherweight, mobile bags in every size, material and style.

Any bag fitted with shoulder or pull straps should allow them to be removed and tucked away safely inside. The reason is they become snagged on conveyor belts and this may send your bag on an unwanted trip into never-never land.

Similarly, bags with double handles should have some type of snap-together closure to bind the two handles together.

TIPS FOR BACKPACKERS

Backpacks are becoming increasingly popular among travelers whatever their mode of transportation. Experienced backpackers warn that a backpack in a store or at your home may seem as light as a feather, but it can become a pain-producing, itchy monster on some hot cobbled street on a summer's day. Before you leave, fill the backpack and take it for a long walk.

Packs with internal frames usually hold up well, even if tossed about by baggage handlers. Packs with external frames distribute the weight better and lift the pack off your back, but can easily become hooked on baggage conveyors. When checking backpacks on airlines or trains, tape the straps to the sides of the pack. Finally, remember that in many countries a backpack is a sign of a foot-loose, wandering camper-type and, therefore, the wearers may not be received as warmly as they might like.

SECURITY AND YOUR LUGGAGE

National news programs have periodically featured stories about so-called "great skyway robberies" occurring at major U.S. airports. There seems no doubt that thievery occurs in poorly guarded baggage handling facilities, even though the Airline Transport Authority claims its records show that only 3 bags in 100,000 have ever been pilfered.

Some bags are fitted with combination or key locks, which may be slight deterrents to would-be thieves. On the other hand, experienced thieves can break open those locks with a quick twist of a knife. Even quicker penetration can be made into soft-sided luggage with a sharp knife, and clasps on hard-sided luggage can be forced open with a small screwdriver. Here are some tips to help discourage theft and loss:

- Carry valuables (such as a jewelry case) with you in your carry-on bags.
- Do use locks as deterrents on checked luggage, but realize they are not sure-fire solutions.
- Expensive, flashy luggage draws attention, so it is best to choose nondescript styles.
- To avoid having other passengers inadvertently take your baggage, mark your cases with some distinguishing mark: a bright strap, a piece of colored yarn on the handle, or colored

tape around or criss-crossing the bag. Bright or not, luggage straps also offer protection if your bag happens to pop open.

- Remember that unattended small bags are easier to grab and snatch than larger ones, so avoid checking them, if possible.

Mark your bags with some distinctive marks or symbols to minimize confusion at baggage claim.

- Always have identification tags on each and every bag. Use the ones with a flap covering your name and address. Another trick is to label your luggage inside the bag as well. Also, place a copy of your itinerary inside so that if the bag is lost and the identification tag is missing, airline officials can track your whereabouts.
- The safest precautions of all are:
  —Make or purchase a canvas cover for your bag with metal rings around the edges, then pass a cable lock through the rings to secure the cover.
  —Or, buy reinforced steel suitcases with the strongest possible locks.

TRAVEL TIP When checking in at airline counters, we all are understandably preoccupied. Veteran travelers, however, always watch airline personnel affix the destination labels to their bags, double-checking that the bags are being sent to the right destination. While many luggage tags are now usually computer-printed instead of hand-selected, it is still possible to make mistakes. ■

PACKING

"Pack half as much as you think you'll need, and then take twice as much money." That's an oft-repeated piece of advice from many modern-day voyagers.

Still, others quickly confess, "I've traveled all over the world for both business and pleasure, and I am still guilty of overpacking." For example, one well-traveled Chicago woman, packing for her husband for a two-week golfing tour of Europe, admitted she packed 14 pairs of golf slacks for him.

Packing a suitcase, whether it be for a short trip of just a few days or for an around-the-world cruise, becomes almost as personal a matter as one's own handwriting. We each have our own twists, turns, and favorite flourishes.

For example, one inveterate business traveler proudly states, "I pack my cases in exactly the same way each time. That way, if necessary, I can locate a specific pair of socks or my trusty flashlight or radio, even in pitch dark."

Another says, "My mental checklist for packing is very simple. I start at the top of my head and work down. That means I start by saying, 'Will I need a hat or scarf?' Then, I assure myself that I have all my personal toiletries (shaving gear, deodorant, prescriptions, toothbrush). Then I work my way down: ties, shirts, suit and sport coats, belts, suit and casual trousers, underwear, socks and shoes—right down the body. Then I say, 'Extras?' That means swimming suit, sports shirt, running shoes, and so on."

Still a third veteran suggests this formula, "Imagine how you'll be spending each day on your trip, or a typical series of four or five days. Try to picture what you'll be likely to wear during those days: Suits? A sport coat? Casual wear? Sweaters? Sports gear? Then, think in terms of combinations and color compatibility. In other words, make sure everything coordinates. For example, I may decide to stick with basic blues and greys, so then I make certain every other item coordinates with blues and greys. That way, I don't have to take brown shoes, or extra ties to complement one brown combination."

Whatever your trick, or choice, or idiosyncrasy, here is a list of ideas and suggestions for packing efficiently. One or several of these may become one of your favorites:

• Pack heavy items (shoes, hair dryer, camera, pocket radio) around the perimeter of a bag, especially along the bottom side. Otherwise, these heavy items move around and crease the softer items.

• Pack smaller items inside your shoes, such as socks, handkerchiefs, or plastic bottles. Otherwise, the empty space inside your shoes is just wasted.

• Pack items you think you may need to retrieve like a sweater or jacket last, so they're on the top.

• Make liberal use of those clear plastic bags you receive from the dry cleaners. In fact, start saving them now and build up a supply. Then, use them—especially inside suit bags—for each garment. This will minimize the creasing of clothing, even when folded in a suit bag or suitcase.

• Pack a small, collapsible nylon bag in one of your cases. These can be used for a number of purposes: An extra tote bag when going to the beach, a repository for dirty laundry, an extra conveyance for purchases made along the route, and so on.

• Pack similar pieces in alternate directions to make the pile flatter. Place the neckline of one item at one end of the suitcase, and then place the next item on top of that, with its neckline at the opposite end.

• Unpack your suitcase as soon as you get to your destination so your clothes won't stay for long periods in a suitcase, accumulating wrinkles. If you do find wrinkled pieces, use the "steam room" method: Hang your clothes on the shower curtain rod and fill the tub with hot water. Close the bathroom door and let the steam eliminate at least some of the wrinkles.

• Put all liquids in plastic bottles and then into separate plastic bags. Reduce risks of leakage by squeezing such bottles slightly as you put on the top. It removes the bubble of air that expands at higher altitudes and that, in turn, causes leakage. You can also reinforce the top with tape.

• Keep an eye out for gift-with-purchase specials at local department stores if you have a favorite perfume or cologne. With these specials, when you buy a bottle of fragrance, you receive a bag with travel-size samples of the fragrance and items like soap, deodorant, moisturizer, and bath gel. They're great for traveling.

• Use empty 35-millimeter film containers or hard matchboxes to carry tiny items like safety pins, rubber bands, and paper clips.

• Some taboos when packing: Lighter fuel is not permitted on an aircraft. Knives may be confiscated from your hand-luggage. Open liquor bottles may be confiscated or sealed with tape. Aerosols and some fountain pens may leak if the baggage compartment is not sufficiently pressurized.

WHAT CLOTHING TO PACK?

Answers to this question depend on the type of trip you're taking, how long you will be away, and what type of climate(s) you will be encountering. It is possible to offer some general suggestions:

• First, unless you always send everything that's soiled to the dry cleaners, find out if you will have access to a washer and dryer. Even the finest cruise ships have do-it-yourself laundry facilities. Then make sure the majority of your clothing is wash-and-wear. This trick can cut down on the quantity of clothing you need to pack.

• Don't wait until the last minute to pack. The wise traveler will start several days prior to departure by laying out items by groups: underwear, shirts, blouses, suits, dresses, accessories, sports wear, shoes, and so on. By spreading everything out, it's possible to see where there may be gaps or duplications.

• Make sure the clothes you pack are adequate for the weather of your destination. Most guidebooks provide temperature ranges, by month, for every region of the world. A faster route might be to watch the cable news programs that often carry weather conditions in every hemisphere and region. Lacking either of these, just ask your travel agent for climate information on your destination.

• Take along a raincoat. In summer, a raincoat that folds into a slim pouch is a wise precaution. For other seasons, a raincoat with a zip-out lining protects you under varied conditions.

• Be prepared for cold weather. If you are concerned that a snap of cold weather might catch you, but you don't want to take along a heavy winter coat, take a coat with a zip-out lining. Be sure to coordinate your wardrobe so that you can utilize the "layered look." Several layers of clothing under even a thin raincoat are just as effective as a single, winter-weight outer garment.

• Avoid the temptation to "go native," that is, buying all the trappings of the culture you'll be visiting. Yes, camping-type clothes are good for safaris, and beach clothes are good for white sandy beaches, but don't worry about advance purchases of barong tagalogs for the Philippines or guyabaras for Central America. Wait until you arrive there to see what might be appropriate. As for formal clothes, they are necessities for some cruises or if your agenda specifically calls for formal dress events. Even then, for men at least, formal attire can usually be rented in major cities abroad.

• Plan your outfits around neutral colors like black, navy, grey, and camel in easy-to-pack fabrics like silk and wool gabardine. Separates always work well in these colors because you can create endless combinations. If a piece of clothing doesn't go with at least two other items in your suitcase, don't pack it.

TRAVEL TIP The best, single basic rule regarding colors and styles is: Be conservative. Well-tailored, conservative styles in good fabrics are fashionable anywhere, whether male or female. ■

• Take only three pairs of shoes—wear one pair, and pack the other two. One pair should be formal to go with any suit or dressy dress. The second pair should be casual, comfortable walking shoes. The third pair might be athletic shoes for walking or other exercise.

• Avoid sleeveless shirts, tank tops, and short-shorts when visiting religious shrines. Sometimes it is customary—even required—that heads, arms, and thighs of both men and women must be covered. That means women should carry an all-purpose silk scarf.

On the subject of laundry, overnight service for laundry and dry cleaning is usually available at good hotels in all major capitals of the world (and aboard better cruise ships), but such "rush" service can be very costly and there may be extra delays on weekends. Therefore, when you find it is time to have laundry done, send it immediately on arrival at your hotel to allow ample time (two or three days) for its return at the lowest cost.

PREPARING A CARRY-ON SURVIVAL KIT

Here is a suggested list of "survival" items to include in your carry-on luggage. The objective is to be able to cope for several days in the event your checked luggage is misrouted or (alas!) lost.

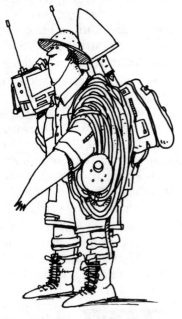

• Passport, traveler's checks, and airline ticket;
• Valuables, such as jewelry;
• Reading material (paperbacks weigh far less, and most public libraries have reasonably good selections);
• Motion-sickness and pain medicine, as well as sleeping aids;
• All prescription medicines packed in their original bottles;
• A small penlight, ballpoint pen, and perhaps an extra pair of eyeglasses or sunglasses;

Preparing a "survival kit" is essential for any trip, but be careful not to overdo it.

- A small tube or plastic bottle of sunscreen;
- Band-aids;
- Eye mask, ear plugs, and an inflatable neck pillow;
- An antacid, plus diarrhea remedies;
- An all-purpose antibiotic salve or cream;
- A toothbrush and toothpaste;
- Deodorant;
- Shaving gear;
- Some "handi-wipe" packs;
- A folding or collapsible umbrella; and
- A small travel alarm clock.

Finally, many experienced travelers also include a bathing suit, a change of underwear, and one extra change of clothes. Some women also include their complete makeup kit within their carry-on luggage.

WHAT TO WEAR EN ROUTE

"Dressing up" for the trip to your destination is out of date. Now, almost anything goes . . . as long as it's comfortable and not offensive to others. For women, "sweater" separates work well because they are soft, don't wrinkle excessively, and can be used in combination with the other clothes. Women should wear flat, comfortable shoes and avoid taking them off on the airplane because feet tend to swell on long flights. For men, ties are a requisite only if you expect to be met at the airport by your business colleagues for immediate business affairs.

WHAT TO DO ABOUT DAMAGED OR LOST LUGGAGE

If you find your luggage is damaged, follow these four steps:

1. Immediately take it to the airline baggage office. They are usually located near the baggage claim area. Even during late-night hours, there should be some official available to take reports of damaged or lost luggage.
2. Point out all the damage, including any items that have fallen out of your suitcase as a result of a tear or puncture in the bag.
3. The airline baggage official will then explain your options. Options may include a voucher or approval form for repair or cleaning at the expense of the airline. Or, they may provide an allowance for purchase of a new bag and/or its contents.
4. The airline is obliged to deliver your luggage to you in the same condition it was entrusted to them. If the agent tries to

depreciate the value because of age of the luggage, resist. As travel writer Jack Cummings says, "(Argue) that you didn't pay less for your ticket because you flew on a 15-year-old aircraft rather than a new one."

In the event your luggage is lost or misrouted, follow these five steps:

1. After making absolutely certain your luggage has not been delivered with other bags on your flight, report the loss to the baggage claim office. (*Note:* This is where it is essential that you are able to show the agent your baggage claim stubs. Do not relinquish those stubs; they become your legal claim for return or recompense.)
2. You will likely be asked to review a pictorial form showing the shape and size of various types of luggage, and you should do your best to point out which drawing resembles your bag and provide any further description.
3. Ask what provisions are made by the airline to tide you over until the luggage is returned. Some airlines have temporary travel kits available; others will provide vouchers or allowances for the purchase of certain necessities.
4. If after 24 hours have elapsed, you are required to purchase incidentals (shampoo, toothbrushes, etc.), you can start billing the airline for between $30 to $50 a day (for up to three days), provided you have receipts.
5. If you believe you are being treated poorly or inefficiently, ask to see the baggage claim department manager. Be forthright and insistent, but calm and unemotional—and avoid making unreasonable demands.

Finally, bear in mind that "lost" luggage is usually either misplaced or misrouted and will turn up and be delivered to you . . . eventually. Try to chalk it up to just one of the many hazards of world travel. Remember that more people are traveling today than at any previous time in history.

If the prospect of lost luggage is of great concern to you, public records are available showing rates of losses for each major airline. Ask your travel agent for that information before booking your ticket.

Also, see Chapter 11 on insurance to learn how to protect the value of your luggage while traveling.

A COMPREHENSIVE CHECKLIST FOR PACKING

For Men

- ☐ Hat(s)
- ☐ Topcoat
- ☐ Scarf
- ☐ Raincoat
- ☐ Rubbers
- ☐ Tuxedo and accessories
- ☐ Suit(s)
- ☐ Sport coat(s)
- ☐ Trousers
- ☐ Sport slacks
- ☐ Casual slacks
- ☐ Sweater(s)
- ☐ Belt(s)
- ☐ Suspenders
- ☐ Neckties
- ☐ Dress shirts
- ☐ Collar pins
- ☐ Collar stays
- ☐ Cuff links
- ☐ Casual shirts
- ☐ Golf/tennis/sport shirts
- ☐ Walking/golf shorts
- ☐ T-shirts
- ☐ Undershirts
- ☐ Underpants or briefs
- ☐ Long underwear
- ☐ Dress socks
- ☐ Sport socks
- ☐ Shoes (dress, walking, sport)
- ☐ Handkerchiefs
- ☐ Bathrobe
- ☐ Swimsuit
- ☐ Slippers
- ☐ Thongs

For Women

- ☐ Mix and match:
  - ☐ Skirts
  - ☐ Blouses
  - ☐ Sweaters
  - ☐ Jackets
  - ☐ Slacks
- ☐ Warmup suit
- ☐ Bathing suit (cap)
- ☐ Cover-up
- ☐ Cocktail dress/pants
- ☐ Dressy blouse
- ☐ Dress shoes
- ☐ Walking shoes
- ☐ Sport shoes
- ☐ Lingerie
- ☐ Pajamas
- ☐ Lightweight robe
- ☐ Travel slippers
- ☐ Knit shirts (long, short sleeve)
- ☐ Walking shorts
- ☐ Sport shorts
- ☐ Travel purse
- ☐ Dress purse
- ☐ Sun hat or visor
- ☐ Thongs
- ☐ Pantyhose
- ☐ Knee highs
- ☐ Sport socks
- ☐ Footies
- ☐ Scarves
- ☐ Make-up
- ☐ Jewelry
- ☐ Top coat
- ☐ Raincoat (zip-out liner)
- ☐ Gloves

Miscellaneous

- ☐ Extra eyeglasses (or contacts)
- ☐ Flashlight
- ☐ Swiss army knife
- ☐ Sewing kit
- ☐ Handiwipes
- ☐ Signal mirror
- ☐ Thermometer
- ☐ Laundry kit
- ☐ Travel umbrella
- ☐ Immersion heater
- ☐ Portable coffee maker
- ☐ Radio, cassette player, or CD player
- ☐ Stain remover
- ☐ Hair dryer
- ☐ Curling iron/brush
- ☐ Voltage converter
- ☐ Shoe horn
- ☐ Travel iron/steamer
- ☐ Pocket calculator
- ☐ Post cards
- ☐ Stationery
- ☐ Pens/pencils
- ☐ Language dictionary
- ☐ Assorted gifts
- ☐ Journal or diary
- ☐ Travel alarm clock
- ☐ Miniature clip-on book light
- ☐ Jump rope (or other exercise equipment)
- ☐ Wrinkle remover spray
- ☐ Camera/film
- ☐ Money belt or pouch
- ☐ Door lock
- ☐ Ziploc storage bags
- ☐ Toiletries
- ☐ Tobacco/cigarettes
- ☐ Reading material
- ☐ Inflatable pillow
- ☐ Eye mask
- ☐ Sports gear (tennis racket et al.)

And, finally the **three most essential** *items:*

- ☐ Passport
- ☐ Tickets
- ☐ Money

Appendix A

Additional Reading

Today's traveler has a rich supply of reading resources for information and help. As we have stated repeatedly, your first stops should be at your local library and bookstores for books dealing with the whole spectrum of world travel.

There are also numerous catalog and publishing houses, and newsletters, that deal with traveling abroad. Here are a few we have found to be especially helpful.

• **Intercultural Press, Inc.** This is both a publisher and distributor of books dealing with cross-cultural subjects from every part of the globe. You'll find such titles as *Good Neighbors, Communicating with Mexicans* (John C. Condon), *Understanding Arabs* (Margaret Kleffner Nydell), *Spain Is Different* (Helen Wattley Ames), *Subject: India* (Jennifer Ladd), *Breaking the Language Barrier* (H. Douglas Brown), along with separate book listings for international business and cultural education. For free copies of periodic catalogs, contact Intercultural Press, Inc., P.O. Box 700, Yarmouth, ME 04096, (207) 846-5168, fax (207) 846-5181.

• **Book Passage.** This is both a mail order and retail store that specializes in travel books. Its 48-page annual catalog is crammed with books on every conceivable facet of overseas travel. All of the popular series travel guides bearing names like Fodor, Frommer, Birnbaum, Michelin, Berlitz, Insight Guides, and Cadogan are included, plus many more. Language tapes and books also take up several pages in the catalog, where you'll even find mystery novels set in overseas locales. Elaine Petrocelli is the charming and dynamic president of Book Passage located north of San Francisco. For a copy of the Book Passage Catalog, or to order books, call (800) 321-9785. The address is 51 Tamal Vista Blvd., Corte Madera, CA 94925.

• **The Literate Traveller.** This is a catalog for, just as the title implies, those readers whose interest in world travel goes beyond merely the top ten tourist attractions in each major city. A 45-page annual catalog lists separate sections devoted to books about the main geographic regions of the world and also to such specialized interests as traveling with the disabled, family travel, mature travel, rail travel, travel classics, and travel humor. Just skimming the unique titles in the catalogs will stimulate your interest and convince you that there is more to travel than just airplanes, hotels, and tour guides. For example, you'll find books for travelers with focused interest in history, art, gardens, music, waterways, walking tours, foods, railroads, and even several books just on dinosaurs. You can receive a catalog for $2 by writing The Literate Traveller, 8306 Wilshire Boulevard, Suite 591, Beverly Hills, CA 90211. To place orders, call (800) 850-2665, fax (310) 398-8781.

• **The Pelican Publishing Co.** offers a smaller collection of travel books than any of the aforementioned sources, but offers some intriguing subjects. For instance, two books are offered just on golf courses in Europe. A separate series, called *The Maverick Guide Series,* appeals to the more adventuresome traveler and includes separate books on Australia, New Zealand, Berlin, Bali, Thailand, Malaysia and Singapore, Prague, Vietnam, Laos, and Cambodia. Bed & breakfast inns for Australia and New Zealand have separate books. To obtain a catalog, contact Pelican Publishing Co., P.O. Box 3110, Gretna, Louisiana 70054, (504) 368-1175, fax (504) 368-1195.

• **The Network for Living Abroad** is a monthly newsletter advertised as providing "news, views, resources, and networking for internationally aware individuals." Each issue spotlights a particular country with descriptions on living conditions there as well as providing updates and tips on various other regions around the world. Subscriptions cost $36. Write "Living Abroad," 13351-D, Riverside Drive, Suite 101, Sherman Oaks, CA 91423.

• **CULTURGRAMS** have been mentioned elsewhere in this book but deserve repeated recognition. This series of four-page newsletters, one for each of 100 different countries, provides extremely useful information about the people of those countries. Insights are provided into local greetings, conversational taboos, family life, the local language, eating and dining habits, plus the demographics and history of that country. A list of recommended reading is also provided. This information has been carefully compiled by young missionaries from the Church of the Latter Day Saints who travel the globe visiting both urban and rural homes. The results of their experiences have then been published by Brigham Young University. For information on purchasing a full set of CULTURGRAMS, write to: David M. Kennedy Center Publications, P. O. Box 24538, Brigham Young University, Provo, Utah 84602-4538, (800) 528-6279. Also, request a complete catalog of other publications offered by this Center.

Appendix B

Tourist Information Offices
around the World*

ALBANIA. Mission of the Republic of Albania, 320 E. 79th St., New York, NY 10021, (212)249-2059.

ALBERTA. Alberta Economic Development and Tourism, City Centre Building, 10155 102nd St., Edmonton, Alberta T5J 4L6, Canada, (800)661-8888.

ANDORRA. The Legation of the Principality of Andorra, 73-27 193rd St., Fresh Meadows, NY 11366, (718)468-3060.

ANGUILLA. Anguilla Tourist Information Office, c/o Medhurst & Associates Inc., 271 Main St., Northport, NY 11768, (800)553-4939.

ANTIGUA, BARBUDA. Antigua and Barbuda Department of Tourism, 610 Fifth Ave., Suite 311, New York, NY 10020, (212)541-4117.

ARGENTINA. Argentina Government Tourist Information, 12 W. 56th St., New York, NY 10019, (212)603-0443.

ARUBA. Aruba Tourism Authority, 1000 Harbor Blvd., Weehawken, NJ 07087, (800)862-7822.

AUSTRALIA. Australian Tourism Commission, 489 Fifth Ave., 31st Floor, New York, NY 10017, (212)687-6300.

AUSTRIA. Austrian National Tourist Office, 500 Fifth Ave., Suite 2009, New York, NY 10110, (212)944-6880.

BAHAMAS. Embassy of the Bahamas, Tourism Division, 2220 Massachusetts Ave. NW, Washington, DC 20008, (202)319-0004 or Bahamas Tourist Office, 150 E. 52nd St., 28th Floor, New York, NY 10022, (800)627-7281.

BARBADOS. Barbados Board of Tourism, 800 Second Ave., 17th Floor, New York, NY 10017, (800)221-9831.

BELGIUM, Belgian National Tourist Office, 745 Fifth Ave., Suite 714, New York, NY 10151, (212)758-8130.

BELIZE. Caribbean Tourism Organization, 20 E. 46th St., Fourth Floor, NY 10017, (212)682-0435. Embassy of Belize, 2595 Massachusetts Ave. NW, Washington, DC 20008, (202)332-9636.

BERMUDA. Bermuda Department of Tourism, 310 Madison Ave., Suite 201, New York, NY 10017, (800)223-6106.

BOLIVIA. Embassy of Bolivia, 3014 Massachusetts Ave. NW, Washington, DC 20008, (202)483-4410.

BONAIRE. Bonaire Tourism Office, 201 1/2 E. 29th St., New York, NY 10016, (212)779-0242.

*© 1993, *The Washington Post*. Reprinted with permission.

BOTSWANA. Embassy of the Republic of Botswana, 3400 International Dr. NW, Suite 7M, Washington, DC 20008, (202)244-4990.

BRAZIL. Brazilian Embassy, Cultural Section, First Floor, 3006 Massachusetts Ave. NW, Washington, DC 20008, (202)745-2804.

BRITISH COLUMBIA. Tourism British Columbia, Ministry of Tourism, Parliament Building, Victoria, B.C. V8V 1X4, Canada, (800)663-6000.

BRITISH VIRGIN ISLANDS. B.V.I. Tourism Board, 370 Lexington Ave., Suite 416, New York, NY 10017, (212)696-0400 or (800)835-8530.

BULGARIA. Balkan Holidays USA, 41 E. 42nd St., Suite 508, New York, NY 10017, (212)573-5530.

CANADA. There is no main Canadian tourism office; see listings for individual provinces.

CAYMAN ISLANDS. Cayman Islands Department of Tourism, 420 Lexington Ave., Suite 2733, New York, NY 10170, (212)682-5582.

CHILE. Chilean Embassy, 1732 Massachusetts Ave. NW, Washington, DC 20036, (202)785-1746.

CHINA. Embassy of People's Republic of China, 2300 Connecticut Ave. NW, Washington, DC 20008, (202)328-2517, or the China National Tourist Office, 60 E. 42nd St., Room 3126, New York, NY 10165, (212)867-0271.

COMMONWEALTH OF INDEPENDENT STATES. Intourist, 630 Fifth Ave., Suite 868, New York, NY 10111, (212)757-3884.

COSTA RICA. Costa Rica National Tourist Bureau, 1101 Brickell Ave., Suite 801, Miami, FL 33131, (800)327-7033.

CURACAO. Curacao Tourist Board, 400 Madison Ave., Suite 311, New York, NY 10017, (800)332-8266.

CYPRUS. Cyprus Tourism Organization, 13 E. 40th St., New York, NY 10016, (212)683-5280.

CZECHOSLOVAKIA. Cedok, Czechoalovak Travel Bureau Inc., 10 E. 40th St., Suite 3604, New York, NY 10016, (212)689-9720.

DENMARK. The Danish Tourist Board, 655 Third Ave., New York, NY 10017, (212)949-2333.

DOMINICA. Dominica Tourist Office, c/o Caribbean Tourism Organization, 20 E. 46th St., Fourth Floor, New York, NY 10017, (212)682-0435.

DOMINICAN REPUBLIC. Dominican Republic Tourist Board, 1 Times Square, 11th Floor, New York, NY 10036, (212)768-2480.

ECUADOR. Ecuador Tourism Office, 1390 Brickell Ave., Third Floor, Miami, FL 33131-3324, (800)553-6673.

EGYPT. The Egyptian Government Tourist Office, 630 Fifth Ave., 17th Floor, New York, NY 10011, (212)332-2570.

EL SALVADOR. Embassy of El Salvador, 2308 California St. NW, Washington, DC 20008, (202)265-9671.

ESTONIA. Embassy of Estonia and Permanent Mission of Estonia to the United Nations, 630 Fifth Ave., Suite 2415, New York, NY 10111, (212)247-1450.

EUROPE. European Travel Commission, 630 Fifth Ave., Suite 565, New York, NY 10111, (212)307-1200.

FINLAND. The Finnish Tourist Board, 655 Third Ave., New York, NY 10017, (212)949-2333.

FRANCE. French Government Tourist Office, 610 Fifth Ave., New York, NY 10020, (900)990-0040 (50 cents a minute).

GERMANY. German National Tourist Office, 122 E. 42nd St., 52nd Floor, New York, NY 10168-0072, (212)661-7200.

GREAT BRITAIN. British Tourist Authority, 551 Fifth Ave., Seventh Floor, New York, NY 10176, (212)986-2200.

GREECE. Greek National Tourist Organization, 645 Fifth Ave., Fifth Floor, New York, NY 10022, (212)421-5777.

GRENADA. Grenada Tourist Office, 820 Second Ave., Suite 900D, New York, NY 10017, (800)927-9554 or (212)687-9554.

GUADELOUPE. French West Indies Tourist Board, 610 Fifth Ave., New York, NY 10020, (900)990-0040 (50 cents a minute).

GUATEMALA. Embassy of Guatemala, 2220 R St. NW, Washington, DC 20008, (202)745-4952 ext. 100.

HAITI. Embassy of Haiti, 2311 Massachusetts Ave. NW, Washington, DC 20008, (202)332-4090.

HONDURAS. Embassy of Honduras, 3007 Tilden St. NW, Washington, DC 20008, (202)966-7702.

HONG KONG. Hong Kong Tourist Association, 590 Fifth Ave., Fifth Floor, New York, NY 10036, (212)869-5008.

HUNGARY. IBUSZ, Hungarian Travel Co., 1 Parker Plaza, Suite 1104, Fort Lee, NJ 07024, (201)592-8585.

ICELAND. The Iceland Tourist Board, 655 Third Ave., New York, NY 10017, (212)949-2333.

INDIA. Government of India Tourist Office, 30 Rockefeller Plaza, North Mezzanine Floor, Room 15, New York, NY 10112, (212)586-4901.

INDONESIA. Indonesia Tourist Promotion Office, 3457 Wilshire Blvd., Los Angeles, CA 90010, (213)387-2078.

IRELAND. Irish Tourist Board, 757 Third Ave., 19th Floor, New York, NY 10017, (800)223-6470 or (212)418-0800.

ISRAEL. Embassy of Israel, 3514 International Dr. NW, Washington, DC 20008, (202)364-5699, or The Israel Government Tourist Office, 350 Fifth Ave., New York, NY 10118, (212)560-0000, ext. 245.

ITALY. Italian Government Travel Office, 630 Fifth Ave., Suite 1565, New York, NY 10111, (212)245-4822.

JAMAICA. Jamaica Tourist Board, 801 Second Ave., 20th Floor, New York, NY 10017, (800)847-4279 or (212)688-7650.

JAPAN. Japan Information and Cultural Center, 1155 21st St. NW, Washington, DC 20036, (202)939-6900, or Japan National Tourist Organization, 630 Fifth Ave., Suite 2101, New York, NY 10111, (212)757-5640.

KENYA. Kenya Tourist Office, 424 Madison Ave., 14th Floor, New York, NY 10017, (212)486-1300.

KOREA. Korea National Tourism Corp., 2 Executive Dr., Seventh Floor, Fort Lee, NJ 07024, (201)585-0909.

LATVIA. Embassy of Latvia, 4325 17th St. NW, Washington, DC 20011, (202)726-8213, or the American Latvian Association, 400 Hurley Ave., Rockville, MD 20850, (301)340-8174.

LIECHTENSTEIN. Swiss National Tourist Office, 608 Fifth Ave., New York, NY 10020, (212)757-5944.

LITHUANIA. Embassy of Lithuania, 2622 16th St. NW, Washington, DC 20009, (202)234-5860.

LUXEMBOURG. Luxembourg National Tourist Office, 801 Second Ave., 13th Floor, New York, NY 10017, (212)370-9850.

MALAYSIA. Malaysian Tourism Promotion Board, 818 W. Seventh St., Suite 804, Los Angeles, CA 90017, (213)689-9702.

MANITOBA. Manitoba Department of Industry, Trade and Tourism, 155 Carlton St., Seventh Floor, Winnipeg, Manitoba R3C 3H8, Canada, (800)665-0040.

MARTINIQUE. French West Indies Tourist Office, 610 Fifth Ave., Suite 222, New York, NY 10020, (900)990-0040 (50 cents a minute).

MEXICO. Mexican Government Tourism Office, 405 Park Ave., Suite 1401, New York, NY 10022, (212)421-6650 or 1911 Pennsylvania Ave. NW, Washington, DC 20006, (202)728-1750.

MONACO. Monaco Government Tourist and Convention Bureau, 845 Third Ave., 19th Floor, New York, NY 10022, (800)753-969 or (212)759-5227.

MONTSERRST. Caribbean Tourism Organization, 20 E. 46th St., Fourth Floor, New York, NY 10017, (212)682-0435.

MOROCCO. Moroccan National Tourist Office, 20 E. 46th St., Suite 1201, New York, NY 10017, (212)557-2520.

NEPAL. Embassy of Nepal, 2131 Leroy Pl. NW, Washington, DC 20008, (202)667-4550.

NETHERLANDS. Netherlands Board of Tourism, 355 Lexington Ave., 21st Floor, New York, NY 10017, (212)370-7367.

NEW BRUNSWICK. New Brunswick Department of Economic Development and Tourism, P.O. Box 12345, Fredericton, New Brunswick E3B 5C3, Canada, (800)561-0123.

NEWFOUNDLAND. Newfoundland Department of Tourism and Culture, P.O. Box 8730, St. John's, Newfoundland A1B 4K2, Canada, (800)563-6353.

NEW ZEALAND. New Zealand Tourism Board, 501 Santa Monica Blvd., Suite 300, Santa Monica, CA 90401, (800)388-5494.

NORTHERN IRELAND. Northern Ireland Tourist Board, 551 Fifth Ave., Suite 701, New York, NY 10176, (212)922-0101.

NORTHWEST TERRITORIES. Northwest Territories Tourism, P.O. Box 1320, Yellowknife, Northwest Territories X1A 2L9, Canada, (800)661-0788.

NORWAY. The Norwegian Tourist Board, 655 Third Ave., New York, NY 10017, (212)949-2333.

NOVA SCOTIA. Nova Scotia Information Center, 136 Commercial St., Portland, Maine 04101, (800)341-6096 or (207)772-6131.

ONTARIO. Ontario Travel, Queens Park, Toronto, Ontario M7A 4R9, Canada, (800)668-2746.

PAKISTAN. Embassy of Pakistan, Information Division, 2315 Massachusetts Ave. NW, Washington, DC 20008, (202)939-6225.

PAPUA NEW GUINEA. The Embassy of Papua New Guinea, 1615 New Hampshire Ave. NW, Washington, DC 20009, (202)745-3680.

PERU. Embassy of Peru, Cultural Affairs Office, 1700 Massachusetts Ave. NW, Washington, DC 20036, (202)833-9860.

POLAND. Orbis, Polish Travel Bureau, 342 Madison Ave., Suite 1512, New York, NY 10173, (800)223-6037 or (212)867-5011.

PORTUGAL. Portuguese National Tourist Office, 590 Fifth Ave., Fourth Floor, New York, NY 10036, (800)PORTUGAL, (800)767-8842 or (212)354-4403.

PUERTO RICO. Puerto Rico Tourism Co., 575 Fifth Ave., 23rd Floor, New York, NY 10017, (800)223-6530 or (212)599-6262.

QUEBEC. Quebec Tourism, 17 W. 50th St., New York, NY 10020, (800)363-7777 or (212)397-0200. Quebec Government Office of Tourism, 1300 19th St. NW, Suite 220, Washington, DC 20036, (202)659-8991.

ROMANIA. Romanian National Tourist Office, 573 Third Ave., New York, NY 10016, (212)697-6971.

SABA. Saba Tourist Information Office, c/o Medhurst & Associates Inc., 271 Main St., Northport, NY 11768, (516)261-7474.

ST. BARTS. French West Indies Tourist Office, 610 Fifth Ave., New York, NY 10020, (900)990-0040 (50 cents a minute).

ST. EUSTATIUS. St. Eustatius Tourist Information Office, c/o Medhurst & Associates Inc., 271 Main St., Northport, NY 11768, (516)261-7474.

ST. KITTS-NEVIS. St. Kitts and Nevis Tourist Information Office, 414 E. 75th St., Fifth Floor, New York, NY 10021, (212)535-1234.

ST. LUCIA. St. Lucia Tourist Board, 820 Second Ave., Ninth Floor, New York, NY 10017, (800)456-3984 or (212)867-2950.

ST. MAARTEN. St. Maarten Tourist Board, 275 Seventh Ave., 19th Floor, New York, NY 10001-6788, (212)989-0000.

ST. MARTIN. French West Indies Tourist Office, 610 Fifth Ave., Suite 222, New York, NY 10020, (900)990-0040 (50 cents a minute).

ST. VINCENT & THE GRENADINES. St. Vincent and the Grenadines Tourist Office, 801 Second Ave., 21st Floor, New York, NY 10017, (800)729-1726 or (212)687-4981.

SASKATCHEWAN. Saskatchewan Tourism, 1919 Saskatchewan Dr., Regina, Saskatchewan S4P 3V7, Canada, (800)667-7191.

SOUTH AFRICA. South African Tourism Board, 747 Third Ave., New York, NY 10017, (800)822-5368.

SPAIN. Tourist Office of Spain, 665 Fifth Ave., New York, NY 10022, (212)759-8822.

SWEDEN. Swedish Tourist Board, 655 Third Ave., New York, NY 10017, (212)949-2333.

SWITZERLAND. Swiss National Tourist Office, 608 Fifth Ave., New York, NY 10020, (212)757-5944.

TAHITI. Tahiti Tourism Board, 300 N. Continental Blvd., Suite 180, El Segundo, CA 90246, (310)414-8484.

THAILAND. Tourism Authority of Thailand, 5 World Trade Center, Suite 3443, New York, NY 10048, (212)432-0433.

TRINIDAD AND TOBAGO. Trinidad & Tobago Tourism Development Authority, 25 W. 43rd St., Suite 1508, New York, NY 10036, (800)232-0082.

TUNISIA. Embassy of Tunisia, 1515 Massachusetts Ave. NW, Washington, DC 20005, (202)862-1850.

TURKEY. Turkish Government Tourism Office, 1717 Massachusetts Ave. NW, Suite 306, Washington, DC 20036, (202)429-9844.

TURKS & CAICOS ISLANDS. Turks & Caicos Islands, P.O. Box 594023, Miami, FL 33159, (800)241-0824.

UKRAINE. c/o Diaspora Enterprises, 220 S. 20th St., Philadelphia, PA 19103, (215)567-7876.

URUGUAY. Uruguayan Tourist Office, 747 Third Ave., 21st Floor, New York, NY 10017, (212)753-8191.

U.S. VIRGIN ISLANDS. USVI Division of Tourism, 900 17th St. NW, Suite 500, Washington, DC 20006, (202)293-3707, or 1270 Avenue of the Americas, New York, NY 10020, (212)582-4520.

VENEZUELA. Embassy of Venezuela, Information and Cultural Service, 1099 30th St. NW, Washington, DC 20007, (202)342-2214.

YUKON TERRITORY. Tourism Yukon, P.O. Box 2703, Whitehorse, Yukon Territory Y1A 2C6, Canada, (403)667-5340.

ZAMBIA. Zambian National Tourist Board, 237 E. 52nd St., New York, NY 10022, (800)852-5998 or (212)308-2155.

Appendix C

Foreign Voltage Guide

Following is a complete and up-to-date guide on voltages in foreign countries. In general, all references to 110V apply to the range from 100V to 160V. References to 220V apply to the range from 200V to 260V. Where 110/220V is indicated, voltage varies within country, depending on location.

A	B	C	D	E
NW-3C	NW-1C	NW-2C	NW-135C	NW-4C

COUNTRY	VOLTAGE	PLUG	COUNTRY	VOLTAGE	PLUG
Afghanistan	220V	B	Lebanon	110/220V	B
Algeria	110/220V	A,B,D	Liberia	110V	A
Angola	220V	B	Libya	110/220V	B
Antigua	220V	D,E	Luxembourg	110/220V	B
* Argentina	220V	D,E	Macao	220V	B
Aruba	110V	A	* Madeira	220V	B
Australia	220V	C	Majorca	110/220V	B
Austria	220V	B	Malawi	220V	D
Azores	110/220V	A,B	Malaysia	220V	D
Bahamas	110V	A	Malta	220V	D,E
Bahrain	220V	D,E	Martinique	220V	B
Bangladesh	220V	B	Mexico	110V	A
Barbados	110V	A	Nepal	220V	B,E
Belgium	110/220V	A,B	Netherlands	220V	B
Belize	110/220V	A	Neth. Antilles	110/220V	A,B,D,E
Bermuda	110V	A	New Caledonia	220V	B
Bolivia	110/220V	A,B	New Zealand	220V	C
Botswana	220V	D,E	Nicaragua	110V	A
* Brazil	110/220V	A,B,C,D,E	Niger	220V	B
Bulgaria	220V	B	Nigeria	220V	D,E
Burma	220V	D,E	Norway	220V	B
Burundi	220V	B	Okinawa	110V	A
Cameroon	110/220V	A,B	Oman	220V	D,E
Canada	110V	A	Pakistan	220V	B
Cen. African Rep.	220V	B	Panama	110V	A
Chad	220V	B	Paraguay	220V	B
Chile	220V	B	Peru	110/220V	A,B
China	220V	B,C,E	Philippines	110/220V	A,B
Columbia	110V	A	Poland	220V	B
Costa Rica	220V	A	Portugal	110/220V	B
Cuba	110V	A	Puerto Rico	110V	A
Cyprus	220V	D,E	Qatar	220V	D,E
Czechoslovakia	220V	B	Romania	220V	B
Denmark	220V	B	St. Lucia	220V	D,E
Dominican Rep.	110V	A	St. Maarten	110/220V	A,B,D,E
Ecuador	110V	A	St. Vincent	220V	D,E
Egypt	220V	B	Saudi Arabia	110/220V	A,B,C,D,E
El Salvador	110V	A	Scotland	220V	D,E
Ethiopia	220V	B	Senegal	110V	B
Fiji	220V	C	Seychelles	220V	D,E
Finland	220V	B	Singapore	220V	D,E
France	220V	B	* South Africa	220V	D,E
French Guiana	220V	B	Spain	110/220V	A,B
Gambia	220V	D,E	Sri Lanka (Ceylon)	220V	E
Germany	220V	B	Sudan	220V	B
Ghana	220V	B,D,E	Surinam	110V	D,E
Gibraltar	220V	D,E	Swaziland	220V	B
Great Britain	220V	D,E	Sweden	220V	B
Greece	220V	B	Switzerland	220V	B
Greenland	220V	B	Syria	220V	B
Granada	220V	B,D,E	Tahiti	110V	A
Guatemala	110V	A	Taiwan	110V	A
Guinea	220V	B	Tanzania	220V	D,E
Guyana	110V	A,B,D,E	Thailand	220V	A,B
Haiti	110V	A	Trinidad	110/220V	A,B,D,E
Honduras	110V	A	Tunisia	220V	B
Hong Kong	220V	D,E	Turkey	110/220V	B
Hungary	220V	B	Turks &		
Iceland	220V	B	Caicos Island	110V	A
* India	220V	B,D,E	Uganda	220V	D
Indonesia	110/220V	A,B,E	Upper Volta	220V	B
Iraq	220V	B	Uruguay	220V	D,E
Iran	220V	B	USA	110V	A
Ireland	220V	D,E	USSR	220V	B
Israel	220V	B	U.S. Virgin Islands	110V	A
Italy	110/220V	B	Venezuela	110V	A
Ivory Coast	220V	B	Vietnam	110/220V	A,B
Jamaica	110V	A	Wales	220V	D,E
Japan	100V	A	Yemen (Arden)	220V	A,B
Jordan	220V	B	Yemen Arab Rep.	220V	B
Kenya	220V	D,E	Yugoslavia	220V	B
Korea	110/220V	A,B	Zaire	220V	B
Kuwait	220V	B,D,E	Zambia	220V	D,E
Laos	220V	B	Zimbabwae	220V	D,E

*Countries using DC in certain areas   Printed in U.S.A.

Appendix D

Travel Bookstores

Before planning your next trip, it would be a good idea to go to your local bookstore or library to read more about your destination. Listed below are just some of the stores that exclusively sell travel books and travel related material.

UNITED STATES

Arizona

The Happy Wanderer
320 N. Highway 89A
Suite H
Sedona, Arizona 86336
(602) 282-4690

California

Easy Going
1400 Shattuck Avenue
Berkeley, California 94709
(415) 843-3533
(415) 843-6725

Geographia Map & Travel
  Bookstore
4000 Riverside Drive
Burbank, California 91505
(818) 848-1414

Perry Supply Co-Maps, Etc.
21919 Sheman Way
Canoga Park, California 91303
(818) 347-9160

Book Passage
51 Tamal Vista
Corte Madera, California 94925
(415) 927-0960

Traveller's Bookcase
8375 West 3rd Street
Los Angeles, California 90048
(213) 655-0575

Thomas Brothers Maps
603 W. Seventh Street
Los Angeles, California 90017
(213) 627-4018

Rand McNally—The Map &
  Travel Store
South Coast Plaza
333 Bristol Street
Costa Mesa, California 92626
(714) 545-9907

Rand McNally—The Map &
  Travel Store
2218 Glendale Galleria
Space H-3
Glendale, California 91210
(818) 242-6277

Rand McNally—The Map &
  Travel Store
Century City Shopping Center
10250 Santa Monica Boulevard
Suite 681
Los Angeles, California 90067
(301) 556-2202

The Travel Store
5612 North Santa Cruz Avenue
Los Gatos, California 95030
(408) 354-9909

Distant Lands
62 South Raymond Avenue
Old Pasadena, California 91105
(818) 449-3220

Phileas Fogg's Books, Maps & More
for the Traveler
87 Stanford South Center
Palo Alto, California 94304
(415) 327-1754

Parmer Books
7644 Forrestal Road
San Diego, California 92120
(619) 287-0693

Professional Travel Consultants, Inc.
P.O. Box 28953 Rancho Bernardo
San Diego, California 92128
(619) 487-9665

Rand McNally—Books &
Travel Store
243 Horton Plaza
San Diego, California 92101
(619) 234-3341

CEC & Associates DBA Export
Resources and World Travel
Society
14 Whaleship Plaza
San Francisco, California 94111
(415) 982-1112

The Complete Traveler
3207 Fillmore Street
San Francisco, California 94123
(415) 923-1511

Rand McNally—The Map &
Travel Store
595 Market Street
San Francisco, California
94105-2803
(415) 777-3131

Travelmarket Book Department
Golden Gateway Commons
130 Pacific Avenue Mall
San Francisco, California 94111

Pacific Travellers Supply
529 State Street
Santa Barbara, California 93101
(805) 963-4438

Easy Going
1617 Locust Street
Walnut Creek, California 94596
(415) 947-6660

The Travel Suppliers
16753 Lake Forest Lane
Yorba Linda, California 92686
(714) 993-7729

Colorado

Pierson Graphics Corporation
899 Broadway
Denver, Colorado 80203
(303) 623-4299

Connecticut

Hannslik & Wegner International
Bookstore
20 Railroad Place
Westport, Connecticut 06880
(203) 454-7750

District of Columbia

Travel Merchandise Mart
1425 K Street, NW
Washington, D.C. 20005
(202) 371-6656

Rand McNally—The Map &
Travel Store
1201 Connecticut Avenue, N.W.
Washington, D.C. 20036

Florida

Rand McNally—The Map & Travel
The Gardens
3101 PGA Boulevard
Palm Beach Gardens, Florida 33410
(407) 775-7602

Hawaii

Rand McNally—The Map &
  Travel Store
Ala Moana Center
1450 Ala Moana 32221
Honolulu, Hawaii 96814

Iowa

Travel Genie
620 West Lincoln Way
Ames, Iowa 50010
(515) 232-1070

Illinois

The Savvy Traveler
50 East Washington
Chicago, Illinois 60602
(312) 263-2100

Rand McNally—The Map &
  Travel Store
150 South Wacker Drive
Chicago, Illinois 60606
(312) 332-2009

Rand McNally—The Map &
  Travel Store
444 N. Michigan Avenue
Chicago, Illinois 60611
(312) 321-1751

Rand McNally—The Map &
  Travel Store
Oakbrook Shopping Center
452 Oakbrook Center
Oak Brook, Illinois 60521
(708) 571-3006

Rand McNally—The Map &
  Travel Store
G101 Woodfield Mall
Schaumburg, Illinois 60173
(708) 995-9606

Louisiana

Travelshelf
3999 South Sherwood Forest
  Boulevard
Baton Rouge, Louisiana 70816
(504) 293-0900

Massachusetts

The Globe Corner Bookstore
One School Street
Boston, Massachusetts 02108
(617) 523-6658

Rand McNally—The Map &
  Travel Store
84 State Street
Boston, Massachusetts 02109
(617) 720-1125

The Globe Corner Bookstore
49 Palmer Street
Harvard Square
Cambridge, Massachusetts 02108
(617) 497-6277

Travelbooks
113 Corporation Road
Hyannis, Massachusetts 02601
(508) 771-3535

Maryland

Rand McNally—The Map &
  Travel Store
Montgomery Mall
7101 Demoncracy Boulevard
Bethesda, Maryland 20817
(301) 365-6277

Travel Books and Language
  Center, Inc.
4931 Cordell Avenue
Bethesda, Maryland 20814
(301) 951-8533

Passenger Stop
Dulaney Plaza
Towson, Maryland 21204

Michigan

Rand McNally—The Map &
Travel Store
Somerset Collection
2801 W. Big Beaver Road,
Space J226
Troy, Michigan 48084-3201
(313) 643-7470

Minnesota

Latitudes
5101 Vernon Avenue South
Edina, Minnesota 55436
(612) 920-1848

Booked
428 Third Avenue NE
Minneapolis, Minnesota 55413
(612) 623-7805

Rand McNally—The Map &
Travel Store
1518 Southdale Center
Edina, Minnesota 55434
(612) 924-0822

Missouri

Rand McNally—The Map &
Travel Store
2423 Saint Louis Galleria
St. Louis, Missouri 63117
(315) 863-3555

Montana

The Official Recreation Guide
Bookshop
100 Second Street East
Whitefish, Montana 59937
(406) 862-4484

New Hampshire

The Globe Corner Bookstore
Settler's Green
Route 16
North Conway, New Hampshire
03860
(603) 356-7063

New Jersey

Map Center
151 Cortland Street
Belleville, New Jersey 07109
(201) 450-8311

Rand McNally—The Map &
Travel Store
The Mall at Short Hills
1200 Morris Turnpike, Suite C123
Short Hills, New Jersey
07078-2724
(201) 379-1800

New York

The Map Man
128 Broadway
Hicksville, New York 11901
(516) 931-8404

British Travel Bookshop
40 West 57th Street, 3rd Floor
New York, New York 10019
(212) 765-0898

The Complete Traveller Bookstore
199 Madison Avenue
New York, New York 10016
(212) 685-9007

Rand McNally—The Map &
Travel Store
150 52nd Street
New York, New York 10022
(212) 758-7488

Traveller's Bookstore
22 West 52nd Street
New York, New York 10019
(212) 664-0995

Ohio

Rand McNally—The Map &
    Travel Store
The Avenue at Tower City Center
230 Huron Road, N.W.
Cleveland, Ohio 44113

The Map Store
5821 Karric Square Drive
Dublin, Ohio 43017
(614) 792-6277

Oregon

Campbell's Bookstore
16155 NW Cornell Road
Beaverton, Oregon 97006
(503) 629-8643

S S Adventure
109 East Fifth
Suite 7
Eugene, Oregon 97401
(503) 485-7348

Pennsylvania

The Traveller's Bookshop
45 East State Street
Media, Pennsylvania 19063
(215) 565-0751

Rand McNally—The Map &
    Travel Store
One Liberty Place
1650 Market Street
Philadelphia, Pennsylvania 19103
(215) 563-1101

Way to Go
4228 Main Street
Philadelphia, Pennsylvania 19127
(215) 483-7387

South Carolina

The Map Shop
5-B East Coffee Street
Greenville, South Carolina 29602
(803) 271-6277

Texas

The Travel Collection
8235 Shoal Creek Boulevard
Austin, Texas 78758
(512) 454-3922

Rand McNally—The Map &
    Travel Store
211 NorthPark Center
Dallas, TX 75225
(214) 987-9941

Rand McNally—The Map &
    Travel Store
Galleria I
5015 Westheimer
Houston, TX 77056
(713) 960-9846

Virginia

Rand McNally—The Map &
    Travel Store
7988 Tysons Corner Center
McLean, Virginia 22102
(703) 556-8688

Washington

Euro-Files
2406 18th Avenue NW
Olympia, Washington 98502-4119
(206) 786-8888

Wide World Books & Maps
1911 North 45th Street
Seattle, Washington 98103
(206) 634-3453

Wisconsin

Going Places Map & Travel
  Bookstore
2860 University Avenue
Madison, Wisconsin 53705
(608) 233-1920

CANADA

Alberta

Journey's Travel Store
315 Eighth Avenue, SW
Calgary, Alberta T2P 4K1
(403) 265-585

British Columbia

Adventure Publishing, Ltd.
3466 W. Broadway, 2nd Floor
Vancouver, British Columbia V6R
  4G8
(604) 731-9958

The Travel Bug
2667 W. Broadway
Vancouver, British Columbia V6K
  2G2
(604) 737-1122

World Wide Books & Maps
736A Granville Street
Vancouver, British Columbia V6Z
  1G3
(604) 687-3320

Earth Quest Books, Ltd.
1285 Broad Street
Victoria, British Columbia V8W 2A5
(604) 361-4533

Ontario

Gulliver's Travel Bookshop
609 Bloor Street West
Toronto, Ontario M6G 1K5
(416) 537-7700

Ulysses Travel Bookstore
101 Yorkville Avenue
Toronto, Ontario M6G 2S2
(416) 323-3609

Quebec

Jet-Setter
66 Laurier Street West
Montreal, Quebec H2T 2N4
(514) 271-5058

Ulysses Travel Bookshop
4176 St. Denis
Montreal, Quebec H2W 2M5
(514) 843-9447

INDEX

Accident insurance, 112–113
Adventure trips, 9–12
Air flight insurance, 109
Air travel, 17–22
  baggage restrictions, 18
  Euro Flyer Pass, 19–20
  helpful publications, 18
  how to save money, 19
  selecting seats, 20–22
Airplane safety, 78–80
Airport limos, 31
Automated teller machines (ATMs),
  61–62
Automobile insurance, 111–112

Backpacks, 121
Baggage insurance, 109–110
Bookstores, travel, 140–145
Business, 102–107
  importance of business cards, 104
  recommended reading, 106–107
  role of U.S. Dept. of Commerce,
    102–104
  tips for trips abroad, 104–106

Car insurance, 111–112
Carnets, in business travel, 105–106
Carry-on luggage, 118–127
Cars, 27–31
Charge cards, 56–57
Child travelers, 13
Clothes, 124–127
  what to pack, 124–125
  what to wear en route, 127
Communication, 96–101
Converters, electrical, 53
Credit cards, 56–57
Cruises, 22–25
  advantages/disadvantages, 23
  dress codes, 24
  gratuities, 24
  selecting, 23–24
  sports activities, 24
Culture, 86–95
  bathrooms of the world, 87–88
  coping with differences, 86–87

  dining, 90–92
  gift-giving, 92–93
  greetings, 89–90
  punctuality, 92
  recommended reading, 95
  tipping, 93–94
Currency, foreign, 59–61
Customs, U.S., 63–65

Damaged luggage, 127–128
Dining around the world, 90–92
Disabled travelers, 13–14
Driving, 27–31
  car safety, 29
  insurance, 29–30
  International Driving Permit,
    29–30
  limos, 30–31
  renting a car, 27–30
Duty free allowances, 64

Elderly travelers, 12–13
Electrical converters, 53
Escorted tours, 5–6
Euro Flyer Pass, 19–20
Explorers' Club, The, 11

Flight insurance, 109
Foreign currency, 59–61
Foreign languages, 96–101
Frequent flyer programs, 19

Gift-giving, 92–93
Greetings around the world,
  89–90

Handicapped travelers, 13–14
Health, 66–75
  avoiding illness, 71–73
  immunizations, 68–69
  jet lag, 74–75
  personal prescriptions, 70
  steps before you depart, 66–68
  what to do if sickness strikes,
    73–74
Hotel safety, 80–81

Illness, 66–75
  avoiding, 71–73
  what to do if it strikes, 73–74
Immunization records, 2
Immunizations, 68–69
Independent tours, 6
Information offices, tourist, 8–9
Institute of Certified Travel Agents,
  4–5
Insurance, 108–117
  accident, 112–113
  automobile, 111–112
  baggage, 109–110
  cancellation/interruption, 110,
    111
  combination policies, 114–115
  different types of, 108–114
  flight, 109
  list of companies, 116–117
  personal effects, 109–110
  sickness, 112–114
  where to start, 115–116
International Driver's Permit, 2,
  29–30
Itineraries, 1

Jet lag, 74–75

Language, 96–101
  how to communicate effectively,
    97–100
  learning foreign phrases, 100–101
Limos, 30–31
Lodging, 42–53
Lost luggage, 127–128
Luggage, 118–130
  backpacks, 121
  carry-on, 126–127
  lost or damaged, 127–128
  security for, 121–122
  types of, 118–121

Magazines, travel, 8
Money, 54–65
  automated teller machines (ATMs),
    61–62
  credit and charge cards, 56–57
  emergency funds, 62–63
  foreign currency, 59–61
  planning for monetary needs, 55

traveler's checks, 57–58
  value-added tax (VAT), 63

Older travelers, 12–13

Package tours, 5–8
  escorted, 5–6
  list of operators, 15-16
  stay-put, 6
  special-interest, 6
  independent, 6
Packing, 118–130
  backpacks, 121
  comprehensive checklist, 129–130
  survival kit, 126–127
  tips for, 122–126
  types of luggage, 118–121
Passports, 2, 32–41
  amending, 38
  applying for, 33–36
  for children, 36
  in an emergency, 36–37
  lost or stolen, 38
  protection, 39
  tourist cards, 41
Personal effects insurance, 109–110
Physically disabled travelers, 13–14
Pickpockets, protection against,
    81–84
Planning the itinerary, 1–16
Postcards, 52–53
Prescriptions, personal, 70
Punctuality, 92

Railroad travel:
  Eurailpass, 25
  tips for, 25–27
  Traveler's Guide, 25
Reading, recommended, 131–132
Rental cars, 27–30
Researching the trip, 2

Safety, 76–85
  on airplanes, 78–80
  before you leave, 76–78
  government publications, 77
  help from the U.S. government,
    84–85
  in hotels, 80–81
  protection against theft, 81–84
  recommended reading, 85

Senior citizen travelers, 12–13
Sickness insurance, 112–114
Solo travel, 8–9
Special-interest tours, 6
Specialty trips, 9–12
Stay-put tours, 6

Theft, protection against, 81–84
Tipping, 93–94
Tourist information offices, 8–9,
    133–138
Transportation options, 17–31
Travel agents, 3–5
    selecting, 3
    steps in choosing, 4–5
    types of, 3
Travel bookstores, 140–145
Travel magazines, 8
Traveler's checks, 57–58

Traveling:
    with children, 13
    with older citizens, 12–13
    with the handicapped, 13–14
Trip cancellation insurance, 110–111
Trip interruption insurance, 110–111

U.S. Customs Office, 63–65
U.S. Department of Commerce,
    102–104
U.S. State Department, 2
    background notes, 2
    tips for travelers, 2
U.S. Tour Operators Association, 7–8

VAT (value-added tax), 63
Visas, 2, 40–41
Voltage guide, 139